SEBASTIAN COE
Coming Back

SEBASTIAN COE
Coming Back

————

David Miller
Foreword by Lord Killanin

SIDGWICK & JACKSON
LONDON

First published in Great Britain in 1984
by Sidgwick & Jackson Limited

ISBN 0-283-99185-2

Typeset by Tellgate Limited, London N6
Printed in Great Britain by
The Garden City Press Limited
Letchworth, Hertfordshire SG6 1JS
for Sidgwick & Jackson Limited
1 Tavistock Chambers, Bloomsbury Way
London WC1A 2SG

Contents

Acknowledgements

A condition of the publication of this book was that Sebastian Coe should win a gold or silver medal in the 1984 Olympic Games, but that is not the only reason for which I owe him thanks. Mainly it is for sharing over the past eight years some of the emotions and thoughts of his successes and failures. Peter Coe, too, has been endlessly informative, and regularly good company. Particular gratitude goes to Lord Killanin, past president of the IOC, for his writing of the Foreword. Since the manuscript had to be with the publisher soon after Seb's final race following the Games, in Zurich, unstinted thanks go to my wife Marita, for her special patience and endurance to direct-type 60,000 words dictation in nine days. Norman Fox, sports editor of *The Times*, who invited me to rejoin the newspaper two years ago, has kindly approved the use of much material published by *The Times*. It is a pleasure to use some of the photographs of Hugh Hastings, who spent many hours recording the more obscure moments of Seb's arduous winter recovery, and of Ian Stewart of *The Times*, whose sensitive eye and lens captured some of the memorable moments in Los Angeles. Once again Mel Watman, editor of *Athletics Weekly* (without which no correspondent should leave home), has consented to the use of extracts from original interviews, by Tony Ward with Peter Coe and by Nigel Whitefield with Peter Elliott. Thanks to Tony Maylam and Drummond Challis of Worldmark Productions for use of material from their documentary *The Supermilers*, and to Neville Holtham of the *Sunday People* for extracts from exclusive interviews by David Barnes with Steve Cram. Coaches such as Len Miller, John Anderson, Frank Dick and Luiz Alberto Oliveira gave generous time and assistance.

Foreword

When Sebastian Coe won the gold medal for the 1,500 metres in Moscow in 1980, as I approached the end of my presidency of the International Olympic Committee, I could not have foreseen that four years later, at the request of my successor, I was to present once again the gold medal for the blue riband of track and field to the same Sebastian Coe. No one could have known then of the fortitude and strength he would require to achieve this double. He had to endure injuries and set-backs that a man of less dedication and courage could not have overcome.

As President of the International Olympic Committee one is at times remote (as indeed are many of the members of the Committee) from the athletes in the many disciplines and sports which are included on the programme of the Olympic and Winter Games. This is due to the necessary bureaucracy for the administration of sport at international and national levels. It was my successor, Juan Antonio Samaranch, who decided to form a permanent Athletes Commission after the Olympic Congress at Baden Baden in 1981, under the chairmanship of Peter Tallberg, a Finnish yachtsman. He was in the unique position of having been a competitor at the Moscow Games in the yachting events at Tallinn, at the same time as being a member of the International Olympic Committee.

When Sebastian Coe found himself addressing the Baden Baden Congress, he had little briefing, but he was extremely articulate. I must admit that I had (and may still have) some reservations about short-circuiting the International and National Federations, but there is no doubt that individual members of this Commission have contributed to a far better understanding between the athletes and the administrators. Sebastian Coe was to make the headlines, especially in the English-speaking press, and to steal the thunder of many of the old bureaucrats at the Baden Baden Congress.

My predecessor, Avery Brundage, always hated the idea of Olympic Congresses. I was in favour of them as a place for an exchange of views between all members of what is loosely termed 'the Olympic family'. This not only includes administrators and athletes but also representatives of the media, as well as those involved professionally or non-professionally in the world of sport, particularly Olympic sports.

I presided over the Congress in 1977 at Varna, where the theme was 'Sport for a World of Peace', and where some reality was introduced into the whole question of eligibility, or what was known as the Amateur Code. For some of the sports which attract money, especially by way of television rights, events may have moved fast. It is inevitable: today it is best to face reality rather than let time stand still. Sebastian Coe helped in this, as indeed he did in his condemnation of the creation of the artificial athlete by drugs and dope, which I always felt was a far greater danger than finance for the athlete, especially when one remembers that the example set by the Olympic and World Champions is followed by the youth of the world. The example set by Sebastian, both as an athlete and a tactician, must be an inspiration, just as the tantrums of some competitors in other sports are a bad example.

Between Moscow and Los Angeles, with their boycott and counter-boycott, I saw Sebastian on several occasions. I remember well discussions held when I was giving the second Noel Baker Lecture (which the late Philip Noel-Baker attended) at Loughborough College, where Sebastian was an economics student. In Los Angeles, when I was visiting the Irish team who were lodged at UCLA near to the British team, I saw him, and was delighted once again to be able to shake his hand and wish him luck. As usual he was on the move, running to his next port of call.

Then came the day when he created Olympic history by winning his second gold medal in the 1,500 metres. Asked by

John Samuel of *The Guardian* what impressed me most about Los Angeles, I said the greatest pleasures were seeing both Chinese peoples competing, the effort made (admittedly a chauvinistic pleasure) by John Treacy of Ireland to gain the silver medal in the Marathon and, above all, Sebastian's victory.

I am delighted that David Miller and Sidgwick & Jackson have had the foresight to publish this book on Sebastian Coe, whose 'coming back' will long be remembered. His place is ensured in the history of the Olympic Games which, despite all the problems which face my successors as presidents, will thrive, I believe – possibly with wise modifications – into the next century.

Killanin

Honorary Life President
International Olympic Committee

Dublin, 1984

Introduction

It was about two in the morning on a sultry night in Rome in September, 1981. Sebastian Coe and I were sitting, having a beer, on the thickly carpeted floor of a hotel in the suburbs. The sofas and easy chairs were over-spilling, as was the bar, with competitors at the World Cup Final – which had just ended at the Olympic Stadium beside the Tiber, where twenty-one years ago Herb Elliott had run his world record 1,500 metres. For Seb, it was the end of yet another spectacular season, his third in succession, which had made him one of the most illustrious figures not just in athletics, but in the sporting world: someone to compare with those who from time to time dominate their field, a Jack Nicklaus, Gary Sobers or Johan Cruyff. Yet, sub-consciously, I was worried for him, so narrow is the dividing line between success and failure which every great athlete must tread as he or she pushes the body to further and further extremes.

On the one hand, I wanted to congratulate him; to impress on this outwardly still modest runner the enormity of the reputation which his exceptional talent had earned him. On the other, as a man some twenty years older, I sensed the need to prepare him for misfortune, to say that life on the track might never again be so sweet, so rewarding, because injury or illness could steal up and drain away his prominence almost overnight. We had a mutual friend who died prematurely earlier that year, who insisted that you should enjoy today because you could not foretell tomorrow. Apart from that one stupid moment of misjudgement and mental eclipse in the 800 metres in Moscow, Seb had known almost nothing but success since the spring day in 1977 when he won the European Indoor 800 metres in San

Sebastian, his first senior international title. I knew by instinct that his luck was unlikely to hold. As we mused over the past twelve weeks – of four world records and a personal best at 1,500 metres (which remains so to this day) – I mentioned my thoughts.

'You've been fortunate, you know, nothing to bother you in the whole season but a serious blister just before the European Cup Final,' I said. 'Nothing in 1980 but a troublesome sciatic nerve which might have put you out of the Olympics but didn't, and a completely clear run in 1979. Your last misfortune was when you fell down a water-hydrant hole before the European Championships in 1978. You have to accept that it probably won't last. Sooner or later you'll run into problems again, and you'd be well advised to adjust *now* to that possibility; to the fact that, although everyone will hope not, you might never again run as brilliantly as you have for the past three years. What you *already* have behind you is an outstanding career.'

Seb nodded, in the dimly lit foyer, as laughing American sprinters tripped over our outstretched legs, and Don Quarrie of Jamaica paused for a word of congratulations. Yes, Seb admitted, it could happen. Yet I sensed that on his present euphoric crest he understandably could not grasp the reality of what I was saying.

It was difficult not to live for the moment. We had just had dinner with his mother, Angela, who had made one of her infrequent trips to see him run overseas, and with the English teacher and his family at whose house Seb had stayed for three months during his warm-weather winter preparation for the Moscow Olympics. Seb was riding one rainbow's end and looking forward optimistically to the next: indeed to the next two or even three. Why not? At twenty-four, age was no impediment. In the 1982 European Championships he would seek to achieve the double at 800 and 1,500 metres, which had eluded him in Moscow, and a month or so after that the same again at the Commonwealth Games in Brisbane; following which he would move upwards to the 5,000 metres, as Dave Moorcroft had done, aiming at the inaugural World Championships in 1983 in Helsinki and, perhaps, the next Olympics in Los Angeles.

Life was indeed good. In 1979 there had been those historic three world records – 800 metres, the mile, 1,500 metres – in forty-one days, which had sent his name rippling around the world on the teleprinters. In 1980 there had been another record, the 1,000 metres, and a silver and gold in his Moscow confrontation with Steve Ovett. Now there had been a season of a world record indoors and three outdoors, including an unparallelled nine days in which Ovett, once, and Seb, twice, had lowered the mile time. He would be elected the first winner of the new Jesse Owens Award, nominated by an international panel of judges from all sports.

Not only was he triumphant on the track: earlier in the week the International Amateur Athletic Federation had approved, under a plan largely devised by representatives of the British Amateur Athletic Board and designed to keep athletics under the control of the international governing body rather than independent pirate promotors and sponsors, the institution of Trust Funds. These would legalize an athlete's acceptance of money from manufacturers and advertisers, provided the finances were administered under the aegis of the athlete's national federation, who would negotiate a cut from the deal to be paid into their own funds for the benefit of the sport. The athlete could draw from the fund for equipment, training expenses, medical facilities and such like, but could not receive the rest of the money until he or she retired from the sport.

Thus Coe and others could now legitimately receive substantial sums as a direct side-benefit from their track prowess, a trend already taking root unofficially in America and elsewhere, and now authenticated by the IAAF. The Soviets and other socialist countries objected, but reluctantly recognized that it was an essential step if the 'amateur' sport was to be kept together under the IAAF roof.

Ironically, it was this officially sanctioned shift towards professionalism, or 'enlightened amateurism' as the cynics called it, which was to bring some of the first winds of adverse publicity in Coe's direction. He had decided to throw in his hand with Mark McCormack's International Management Group, a world-wide agency whose tough-dealing reputation was perhaps unfamiliar with, not to say inexperienced in, the sensitive, controversial and still fluctuating rules of semi-pro athletics. Pro golf was one thing, but athletics was a sport largely new to any businessmen. They might be adept at promoting a deal between a competitor and a shoe manufacturer, but how much did the people at IMG know about the highly specialized requirements of the runner whose fame would project the shoe?

Seb was one of the stars most able to exploit a sport still hypocritically pretending to be amateur, and even more compromised morally in it's attitude to a century's tradition of amateurism in the Olympics – admittedly long since ignored in practice by many sports, with actual encouragement from the Eligibility Commission of the International Olympic Committee. But his association with IMG soon began to make some sections of the press and public slightly cynical about his image as the Mr Right of British sport. It would have been different if he were a full-time professional in an acknowledged professional sport. But in Britain, which has a somewhat perverse idea of fairness, the notion spread, quite unreasonably since he was acting only according to the rules, that Seb was taking an unfair or too smart an advantage.

He was widely and exaggeratedly tipped as the first millionaire of athletics, though some of the American road runners were probably already clandestinely well ahead of him. Yet references to his wealth increasingly appeared in papers such as *The Sunday Times*, and on the eve of the Los Angeles Olympics the *Daily Mail* prefaced their preview of the 800 metres with his alleged 'income of £200,000 a year'. For some, admiration had been replaced by envy. Frank McGhee, long-standing commentator of the *Daily Mirror*, concluded his coverage of Los Angeles with the condemnation that the motto of the Games had now become 'Faster, higher, stronger . . . richer'. Yet this has for a long time been true for medal winners in boxing, skiing or basketball. The only change is that the IOC is now recognizing the inevitable.

I had voiced privately to Seb my reservations about the effect which IMG might have on his public image, never mind his finances, though these were in no way my concern or interest. I could not tell you what he receives for mixing Horlicks in record time, or sweating less in ICI fibres or breaking world records in Oslo or Zurich. That is his affair, and I personally believe that he, or Daley Thompson or anyone else, deserves the money, given the contemporary climate; and I say that as a former member of the training squad for the Olympic soccer team, who believed devoutly in amateurism while it was still a rational ethic.

What I do know is that by nature Seb is not a financial hustler, and if there have been instances when he has seemed to be, then it is probably because of the actions of IMG fulfilling their obligations with vigour on his behalf: sometimes inaccurately reported. He has to contend with the kind of story which appeared in a Sunday paper during the winter of 1981-82, when he stopped driving a Saab Turbo gratuitously provided by the UK distributors. Under the headline 'Seb is pulled up in his tracks', the paper wrote:

Wonder runner Sebastian Coe wasn't satisfied with just having a free Saab to drive around in. He wanted the Swedish car firm to pay him as well. But Saab, I can reveal, stopped our golden boy in his tracks. Not only did they turn down the request, but they took their car back, too. They'd been happy to tax and insure the posh £12,000 turbo saloon and let Coe drive around in it. But pay him too? Oh no.

The trouble began when the rules about what amateur athletes could do by way of promotion were relaxed. Seb signed up with American super-agent Mark McCormack and they tried for a deal involving cash as well as the car. But the demand shook Saab, who had built up a personal relationship with Coe. 'We didn't like it, and asked for the car back the next day' said a spokesman for Saab in Britain.

Mark McCormack's man Robert Jackson explained: 'We look after Björn Borg, who has what we call a full commercial relationship with Saab, and we wanted a similar deal with Seb. He would have been paid and would have been available for commercials, poster-advertising, anything like that. But we couldn't reach an agreement with them.' Not that Seb was reduced to running shoes. He swiftly signed with Hertz, the rent-a-car people, who supply him with a car wherever he happens to be in the world – and pay him.

A mean, slanted and inaccurate story, from a newspaper trying

in 1984 to lure readers with the temptation of million-pound
bingo prizes. Hertz were not paying, and do not pay, for Seb to
drive the car they loan to him. Jackson and IMG were not
involved at any stage with Saab or Hertz and Seb would still be
driving a Saab if the company had not themselves wished to up-
grade the commercial level of Seb's involvement with them. They
asked him to suggest terms, and rejected them, though little
different from the terms any pro golfer would have asked.

I met Jackson in Rome at the time of the World Cup, an affable
but thrusting young man who clearly saw it as part of his
responsibility to help Seb decide where he should run, to
maximize all publicity advantages – which was never Seb's
intention. The decision to join IMG was probably as much
Peter's as Seb's. Peter, a self-made, intelligent and analytical
man, has always believed in the principle that, if possible, you
should go for the best, to the top. Certainly IMG would make
more money more quickly for Seb than anyone else, but would
they enhance his image in a muddled amateur sport? Coe's fame
had given him the introduction to men in the City, working with
long-established firms, who handle more money in a week than
IMG do in a year, but they would have had none of the
specialized experience possessed by IMG to exploit the television
and sponsorship deals which were just around the corner.

What Peter found was that he had harnessed his athletic
leopard to a commercial tiger. Neither of them, of course,
objected to the money. Seb has always argued that the full-time
athlete of the modern televised era should be free to accept the
rewards which have become available. I accept that premise,
because the amateur and the successful international performer
are now mutually exclusive in major sports. What has to ensured
is that a handful of leading competitors do not selfishly exploit
the sport and monopolize the big money, a danger of which Seb
himself is well aware, and it is the aim of the IAAF to control the
changes – as has been done in skiing – and not vainly try to
prohibit them, and lose everything, as has happened in boxing.

Peter and Seb have found it difficult to persuade IMG, not to
say some members of the press, that the agent's role must be
exclusively concerned with finances *off* the track and never with

the schedule of the athlete's running. When Permit Meetings became legal in 1982, with athletes allowed to accept appearance money for their Trust Funds, and then when a Grand Prix was planned by the IAAF for 1985, with prize money for accumulated points, Peter said:

> I continually have to emphasize, to everyone, that for the athlete intent upon excellence, money must always be from areas off the track rather than on it: that the greater the track performance the greater the fringe potential. Therefore we *never* contemplate a single race, anywhere at any time, which is not an integral part of Seb's carefully scheduled combination of training and racing designed to achieve ultimate performance.

Athletics can never be golf or tennis, where the star performer can compete for more than a hundred days a year, and fluctuations in the level of performance do not detract from the commercial spectacle, and can even enhance it. But coupled with the controversy over professionalism were the accusations that for three years Coe and Ovett had avoided each other everywhere but in the Olympics. Seb will adamantly insist that, apart from one single race in 1979, they both spent three years trying to get on to the same starting line as each other, without success.

As 1981 became 1982, the affiliated interests of IMG, of British and American television, of the general public, and of Coe and Ovett themselves, tried to get these two foremost runners into head to head conflict for the first time since the Olympics. This confrontation was the main focus of the British season prior to the European Championships in Athens. Yet for a variety of reasons, as this story will relate, the planned series never took place. Ovett, the 1,500 metres record holder, injured his thigh and was not even able to compete in Athens; and Seb, beset first by injury and then illness, finished only with his third consecutive silver or bronze in a major championship over 800 metres – the distance at which he was so much faster than anyone at that time. His failure to win in 1978 in Prague could be blamed on injury and a calculated tactical experiment with Peter. In Moscow he had had only himself and his mind to blame for not winning the gold. Now? He was not sure. Was it lack of fitness, again caused by injury early in the season, or illness, in the form of glandular fever? Or was he actually slipping? He scratched from the 1982 Commonwealth Games, and had hospital tests instead, before beginning another arduous winter's preparation for the forthcoming World Championships. Any move to the 5,000 metres had to be postponed another year.

Early 1983 began well. Two blistering indoor world records whetted his own and the public's appetite for the summer. But summer brought only renewed anxiety. Apart from a characteristically sharp performance in Oslo, one defeat followed another. Each time some reason could be found, some explanation given, as father and son tried to rationalize their dilemma. Accumulatively the series of set-backs provided only one possible answer, which they were both reluctant to contemplate: Seb was sick.

The ultimate reverse came when he finished fourth in a domestic 800 metres behind Steve Cram, a week before the World Championships were to begin. Immediately he went into hospital again: he had to discover if he was ill because he was running too much, or if he was failing because he had contracted some unrelated ailment.

The world's greatest middle-distance runner was out of the Championships, wondering if he would ever run again. In addition, he and his family were hounded wretchedly by gossip, from both press and athletes or coaches who should have known better. The stories gathered: he was over-trained by Peter; there was a personal breakdown between them; he was on stimulant drugs which would not have passed the dope-tests in Helsinki; an endless stream of denegration at a time when he was at his lowest ebb. An understandable resentment welled within him which only another Olympic triumph, a further proof of his undimmed excellence, could dispel.

To see a supreme sportsman ensnared by injury, misfortune or illness is as distressing as watching one of nature's magnificent wild beasts aimlessly pacing back and forth behind the bars of a zoo. No ordinary person can imagine the anguish for someone such as Nikki Lauda, Jim Ryun, Colin Milburn, Barry Sheene,

Colin Bell or, in the Los Angeles Olympics, Mary Decker, to be summarily cut down in their prime, whatever the cause. Lauda, for one, had made an incredible recovery: could Coe recapture his form in time for the Olympics or, indeed, ever?

Misfortune can change a sportsman's or woman's life not just financially but emotionally. For Mary Decker, fraught by her own impatience behind Zola Budd, it may well prove to be both. For Jim Ryun, the greatest middle-distance runner of his era, it was emotional. When Ryun was tripped in his heat of the 1,500 metres at the Munich Olympics in 1972, having taken only the silver behind Kip Keino at altitude in Mexico City in 1968, he found it too much to manage. In Worldmark's documentary *The Supermilers*, released on the thirtieth anniversary of Roger Bannister's first four-minute mile and telling the progress of the world record since that May evening at Iffley Road in Oxford in 1954, Ryun says:

> Munich was a terribly difficult situation for me, not so much because of the fall. A day later they would show the videos, films, that I was indeed fouled. The hard part would come about twenty-four hours later when the International Olympic Committee jury of appeal, having looked at those films, would simply say: 'That's too controversial, we don't want to do anything; come back in four years and try again.' Now I am paraphrasing that a little bit, but in essence that is what they said, and I was angry at that time because I simply couldn't justify the sacrifice that it would require.
>
> It was at that point in my life that I turned to God, and I said Lord I need some help, I need some kind of way to resolve this, and eventually the Lord would show me that I had to forgive those men, which was the most difficult thing I could ever do. It took me months before I could sit down and say OK, I forgive them for what I thought was a very poor decision. And because I was able to do that I can now go back to running and say it is fun again. But right after the Munich Olympics I didn't want anything to do with running for a long time.

Ryun was twenty-five at the time: he would have been twenty-nine had he made the attempt to run at a fourth Olympics in Montreal. Coe was almost twenty-seven when the bottom fell out of his world. To pull out of such a psychological reverse would need a remarkable combination of will-power, dedication and the conviction that recovery was possible. There would be no proof until the moment of truth on a track on the other side of the world a year later.

Such resolution and belief has nothing to do with financial reward. What Seb was to achieve in Los Angeles in 1984 was a triumph of the spirit, and it is that which has re-established him as one of the legendary Olympians of any era. What happened in those seven races between 3 August and 11 August was not just exceptional in athletics history. It was exceptional in man's unending battle with himself.

An integral part of the achievement was Peter's didactic but shrewd analytical assessment of his son's capabilities. It has been an unusual and rare experience for me to be privileged to observe at close hand a partnership probably without precedent in sport. If the talent has been the son's, much of the judgement has been the father's. There were those after Moscow who questioned Peter's competence, and they were misguidedly questioning him even more after the 1983 breakdown, until the evidence of a blood disease was disclosed by the hospital. There is no doubt that as Seb stood on the victory rostrum a year later with a smile of fulfillment, a portion of the reward belonged to that oddly dogmatic yet vindicated and affectionate man just as much beside himself with happiness on the terraces. As Peter revealingly says later in this story, he is more proud of being Seb's coach than of being his father. Parenthood is fairly commonplace, he reflects.

One

Struggling

The anomalies which athletics were in danger of experiencing, through the relaxation by the International Amateur Athletic Federation of its rules on advertising, became apparent early in 1982. In February, ICI Fibres announced that Seb was one of four sportsmen involved in a £250,000 deal. The names of a golfer and a skier were not revealed, but Keke Rosberg, the Finnish motor-racing driver, was known to be one of the four. The deal for Seb, who had already begun a series of Horlicks advertisements on television, would be administered by the British Amateur Athletics Board. The value of the deal to him was not disclosed, but was thought to be around £50,000. It was easy to see how some amateur officials and others could be envious of such a windfall to a 'mere' runner, a sum probably three times greater than most of them would be earning in a year.

The commercial disparities between Coe and Rosberg, on the other hand, were many and obvious: Rosberg's world was one of million-pound racing cars smothered in advertisements, a world of private jets and technological projects; while Seb's was the lonely existence of training alone in Richmond Park or the Derbyshire Peaks and then meeting with a bunch of amateur running friends for a drink at the pub. From now on Seb would be a ready target for insinuation in a sport which has always thrived on rumour as much as on statistics. What would not change was Seb's fundamental attitude to the sport. As he said: 'One thing is sure. Steve Ovett, Daley Thompson, Allan Wells and I all came into athletics for the love of it. There was not a penny on offer then, from anywhere. If we were asked to start out again on the same basis tomorrow, I am sure we all would.

But if someone now says that he can find a way to give us a share of the money we help generate, without damaging the sport, then I see no harm in taking it. Athletics is not my career. I am still heavily involved at university. When I finish running, I shall begin rehabilitating myself to normal life. I will not want to stay in the sport. And certainly I don't want to contemplate trying to live on my name as a former athlete, getting a job that involves smiling and shaking hands simply because I am, you know, that running bloke. Can you imagine anything more humiliating? I would want to use my education in economics and history, and start repaying my friends for the trouble I have caused them in inconveniences during all the years of competition.' For the time being, therefore, he was happy to run in a red, black and yellow ICI vest at all events, apart from British matches or the European and Commonwealth Games.

The next announcement, in front of an explosion of photographic bulbs, was of the long awaited series between Ovett and Coe over three distances: 3,000 metres at Crystal Palace on 17 July, 800 metres in Nice on 14 August, a mile on the Pacific coast at Eugene, Oregon on 25 September. The sponsors at Crystal Palace would be Citizen Watches, the 3,000 being included in the match between England, Spain, Kenya and Japan. For the first time that anyone could recall, Seb and Steve sat side by side at a press conference and reflected on the fact that victory would not necessarily fall to either of them, because the formidable Henry Rono and Mike Boit of Kenya would be on the starting line, while Americans Steve Scott and Sydney Maree, plus ex-Olympic champion John Walker of New Zealand, would also be there in part of an overall, inter-continental television deal thought to be worth one-and-a-half million pounds in fees and sponsorship.

The conference skated over the question of their fitness. Seb had suffered a stress fracture in the foot, yet Ovett's at this stage was the more questionable following his bizarre collision with some church railings during a training session in Brighton, which necessitated an operation on his thigh muscle. He said he had trained vigorously in the past week and was in better shape than he expected. Both he and Seb said they were glad the race was over 3,000 metres, which would not require too much basic speed – though they needed enough to beat Rono, who held the world record with 7:32.1.

Asked why, when they had not raced each other since Moscow, they chose to start at this particular distance, Seb said: 'Obviously we wanted a range of events, and we're both endurance based athletes, so the 3,000 preferably should come first, even though we wanted to have the first race in front of a British crowd.' Steve said that he was lacking speed in the early part of the season, and therefore could not contemplate beginning with an 800. Obviously the 3,000 suited him, because he held the unofficial two-mile world record. They both said they hoped the importance of the series would be in producing three outstanding races, as much as in providing any definitive answer as to who was the better runner. Ovett said he thought it was an intriguing throw-back to the era of Walter George racing at Stamford Bridge in challenge matches. There were not many things which still motivated him, he said, but this would. Talking subsequently to Colin Hart of *The Sun*, Seb said: 'I certainly wouldn't get any pleasure or satisfaction out of beating Steve if he was only half fit. He must have missed nearly three months of vital winter work, so it wouldn't surprise me if he doesn't make it by July.' In the event, it was Seb who would be the absentee.

Early in June, at the invitation of the French, Seb went to Bordeaux to run 2,000 metres, his only previous race in 1982 having been the usual modest curtain raiser over 1,500 in the Yorkshire Championships at Cudworth. The French press, not to say a few of the English who fancied a trip to the wine country, were quick to label the occasion a world record bid, which was presumptuous. John Walker's time of 4:51.4, set six years previously in Oslo, was a tough objective, and on the day was made no easier by too fast a first lap of under 56 seconds. Tom Wessinghage of West Germany and Craig Masbach of the USA were also disconcerted by the pace-maker. Seb's winning time of 4:58.8 had only ever been bettered in Britain by Ovett, and considering he was still testing reaction to a foot injury, it was more than satisfactory. Yet on returning home Seb found he had a stress fracture of the shin, and had no chance of fulfilling his date with Ovett at Crystal Palace, nor indeed the second meeting at Nice. He was now confronted with a struggle to be in shape in time for the European Championships in September. Enter Steve Cram.

At the end of the previous season, Cram had become the fastest ever twenty-year-old miler when he thrust through the 3:50 barrier on a balmy night in Zurich, but the achievement of the quiet youngster from Hebburn, near Newcastle in the north east, passed without fanfare, because he was a mere third behind another of Seb's world records. In the Moscow 1,500 metres final, still a brilliant student in the shadow of Coe and Ovett, he had been learning; but now in the space of a few weeks he had become a leading contender for the four-lap title in Athens, especially in view of his performance in becoming the third fastest Briton ever over 800 metres, with 1:44.45. Seb, still on the sideline while recovering from his fracture, said of Cram's two-lap time: 'He's right to be improving his speed with this kind of 800. There's no way of avoiding that pace if you are aspiring to the sort of mile or 1,500 now being run by the top men. People are already talking of the end of an era because Ovett and I have had problems. We'll have to wait and see about that, but it's splendid that the challenge is coming as much from within Britain as elsewhere.'

As a twelve year old Cram joined Jarrow and Hebburn, where the club coach was the little-known Jimmy Hedley, a council employee caring for the clubhouse. Hedley was less Cram's coach than his adviser. As Cram said: 'We discuss things all the time, and sometimes we argue like hell. I'm a great believer that too many athletes are too bound by the instructions of their coaches, that you have to react to some extent to your own instincts.' The previous winter he had cut out most of the road racing, started his training later, and had been working on a more intense programme. It had been his intention that, if 1982 did not go well, he would move up to 5,000 metres for the 1984 Olympics, believing that Moorcroft left the switch too late for Moscow after winning the 1978 Commonwealth Games 1,500 metres.

His current form persuaded him that he would stay with four laps at least until 1984. His modesty about his expectation for the European Championships, in which he said he hoped only 'for some sort of medal', stemmed from the fact that he knew Coe and Ovett, if and when fully fit, were still the faster finishers. 'I think the situation now is that they are going to have to be at their best, not just against me but against Scott and Maree and others, to win the big ones. What I do know is that if I am to win, it will have to be with the kind of run which Straub made in the Olympics, a long surge for home over two laps in an attempt to burn off some of the finishing power of the others.' It had been apparent since he reached the Olympic final at nineteen that he was destined one day to succeed Coe and Ovett, but his challenge to their present rule was one of the most exciting prospects in the sport. His 800 metres victory in the Citizen Watches sponsored match upstaged Dave Moorcroft's 3,000-metre victory over an ailing Ovett.

Prior to 1981 Cram had never broken 1:48, and now he achieved the world's fastest time of the year, running from the front. 'I had decided that if I wanted to do anything tonight I'd have to do the work myself,' he said afterwards. He had in mind a first lap of 53, but went through the bell in 51.4, and finished almost two seconds inside his previous best. 'The gap's closed a lot' said Cram prophetically.

What a month it was for Moorcroft! On 7 July, in Oslo, he had come within a stride or so of breaking thirteen minutes for 5,000 metres, and ten days later he came close to overtaking another of Rono's world records. Replacing Coe, who had not yet resumed even jogging, following his stress fracture, and with Rono exhausted and absent after a busy European tour, Moorcroft was offered a challenge only by Maree, out of a field that included Koech and Waigwa of Kenya, Scott and Padilla of America, Walker and Wessinghage . . . and Ovett. The prospect of a new world record almost disappeared with a slow first lap, but steadily Moorcroft built up the pressure, and the opposition, including Ovett, began to wilt. The previous week in Paris, Ovett had dropped out of a race with a stomach upset, and now he soon found himself red-faced and way back. By the final lap there were only two men in it, with Maree challenging Moorcroft down the back straight and inching ahead into the final bend. Down the finishing straight Moorcroft found another kick, and got home by half a second in 7:32.79, inside Brendan Foster's European record of 1974 by 2.5 seconds, and eight-tenths of a second outside Rono's world record. The luckless Ovett plodded in tenth, and though Moorcroft had brilliantly saved the face of Citizen Watches, the projected first major event of the year had been a bit of a non-starter. Now it was a question of whether Coe and Ovett could meet in Nice as scheduled – four days before Coe was hoping to run in Zurich. But pressures of differing kinds were overhauling them: the need to achieve European qualifying times at both 800 and 1,500 metres by 7 August, under the stipulation by British selectors, or at the very latest by 26 August, the official deadline for qualification for the European Championships. Already Seb was hinting that he thought it unlikely he could contemplate a serious race before September. Thus the only possible survivor in the Coe-Ovett series seemed to be the mile in Oregon, after the European Championships. Nothing was certain.

Seb achieved his 800 metres European qualifying time in a specially arranged private trial at the Harvey Hadden stadium in Nottingham during the Loughborough Summer School fortnight. It was organized by the chief national coach, Frank Dick, only eleven days after Seb had resumed training. Seb had been out of action for six weeks, Nice was out of the question, and the purpose of the private trial was as much as anything to prove that he was not unfairly denying a place to another British runner. At this point Seb had decided not to bid for a European place at 1,500 metres, because he was short on time to get fit for even one event. His time in Nottingham was 1:46.5, and was the sort of quiet come-back he needed. Ovett, with continuing problems, had already decided only to go for the 1,500 metres in Athens, but there was the prospect that they would still clash in Oregon, and Brisbane – with BBC television already planning to screen the Commonwealth races live in the early hours of the morning, such was the public interest.

If the Nottingham time solved one problem for Seb, it

immediately created another when Ovett threatened to pull out of the Thorn-EMI Games at Crystal Palace two days later if, would you believe it, Seb was there watching! Apparently Ovett, who was planning to run the 1,500 to achieve his qualifying time, was disgruntled that Seb had been allowed to run *his* in private. In reply to this petty argument, in which the British Board were caught in the cross-fire and at one stage threatened not to accept Seb's private trial even though it had been organized by their own official, Seb said: 'The reason I ran my qualifier privately was that I was unwilling to take part in a meeting which might have encouraged the public to turn up, only for them to be disappointed if I broke down again, which had happened to me recently.'

The Board continued to oscillate, more due to their own indecision than any histrionics from Ovett. It was the latest episode to highlight the difficulties of a major sport, in which technically amateur star athletes can generate huge incomes for the ruling bodies and promotors as well as for themselves, yet receive little sympathy for injury problems. So many ill-informed people had been gunning for Ovett and Coe recently, at a time when neither of them was in a position to answer back, either in print or on the track. They were having to answer the call of federations, selectors, promoters, agents, and a demanding public, as well as the voice of common sense, which often said they ought to be taking it gently.

The insensitivity of the Board, under pressure from a new sponsor, Thorn-EMI, was epitomized by their somewhat unworldly chairman, Dr Bill Evans, who asserted that if Coe could run on Wednesday, he could run on Saturday; besides which, they were not prepared to accept the private trial as a qualifying time 'because the race was not bona fide, as the event was not advertised'. There are times when you would suppose that the Board were there to impede rather than assist its athletes. Seb duly sat in the stands at Crystal Palace to watch Ovett achieve his qualifying time with 3:38.48, and he expressed himself astonished at the news that the Board, who would meet to select the team the following day, could not now consider him to be qualified.

The Board's position was further compromised by the fact
that the European qualifying deadline was 26 August rather than
their own 7 August, and that the Amateur Athletic Association,
responsible for selecting the Commonwealth team for England,
had already announced their selection, including Coe, even
though the Games came after the European Championships. The
Board were trying to assert themselves, but were doing it in a
clumsy way, no doubt some of them with a hidden motive of
wanting to put Coe and IMG in their place. Fortunately for Coe,
he had one or two resolute friends among the selection
committee, and on the Monday it was announced by Dr Evans
that they had given Coe until the official deadline of 26 August to
prove his fitness and again reach the qualifying time; failing
which, Ovett would be asked to double up at both distances. It
may all have been a storm in a teacup, but the argument included
other athletes who were under the same threat, such as Allan
Wells, Daley Thompson and Kathy Smallwood, who also upset
the sponsors by their non-appearance on the Saturday.

Wells claimed he was not fit; Thompson was assisting Essex
Beagles, who were threatened with extinction at the time; and
Smallwood had orders from her doctor not to run, which the
Board would not accept, summoning her to London and
immediately being given the same diagnosis of a thigh injury by
their own doctor, who also said not to run. Glad to shake off the
dust of such an Alice-in-Wonderland controversy, Coe headed
off for a week's training in Switzerland, only to fall foul of an
even more unexpected incident.

Four days before he was due to run an 800 metres in Zurich, he
was spending an afternoon with his parents and a friend, Irene
Epple, the West German skier, at an hotel in Interlaken on the
shore of Lake Thun. Irene returned from a sail-board ride, and
while she was changing out of her wet suit, an argument
developed between Ralph Baumann, a sail-board instructor, and
Seb and his father. Baumann, it seems, complained about where
Irene had left her sail-board, threw it back in the water, and
started to jostle the sixty-three-year-old Peter. At this point Seb
intervened, struck Baumann with a piece of wood to protect his
father, and himself received several punches on the nose. Peter

ended up in the water, Baumann with a cut in his head which needed five stitches, and Seb, after appearing in a Swiss court with a severely bruised nose, with a claim for £160 for medical expenses from Baumann. Out of one teacup into another.

The row duly subsided, both parties swallowed their pride and Herr Baumann his alleged costs, and three days later Seb arrived in Zurich for a further effort to prove that he was ready for Athens. Peter was confident, for all his son's swollen nose, that training performances on Monday had been encouraging, and that they could afford the risk of a reasonably sharp race, with the further intention of returning to run in the Talbot Games at Crystal Palace two days later. 'If Seb is pushed tomorrow, I'm optimistic he can respond,' said Peter. 'I think he can run around 1:45. We've doubled the training which we had during the week of the Nottingham race, and he should now be that much better. On the one hand, if he's to compete in Athens we cannot allow him to get race-rusty, yet we know it only needs another set-back to worry the selectors.' Seb said that he had felt a bit groggy after sitting for half a day in the magistrate's court on Monday, but was now fine. 'If things continue as they are now, then the mile against Ovett, Scott and Maree in Oregon is still on, and I'll be going flat out for the double in Brisbane.'

Within half an hour on the Wednesday night, British middle-distance running reasserted its dominance of international competition when first Coe, and then Cram, bought a full house at the Weltklasse meeting to its feet. For Seb, it was a particularly rewarding evening in a stadium where he had set two world records in the past three years. Up in the stands there were tears of relief from Irene, whose own career on the ski slopes had taught her better than most the fluctuations and pressures which can be exerted on a champion. It was a supreme run by Seb, ghosting away from an impressive pack toward the end of the race.

From the lane-break after the first bend, a burst of speed carried Coe to a secure position on the second bend, and a first lap of 51.5 behind the pace-maker, Koskei of Kenya, was an indication of a fast time. On the second back straight, just as it seemed he might be overhauled, he accelerated clear again,

sprinted into the finishing straight well ahead, and won by five
metres, easing up after the usual backward glances, in 1:44.48.
He was not being falsely modest when he described the race to a
Swiss journalist as 'just a gentle run, being fairly careful'. It was
the second fastest of the year, three-hundredths outside Cram's
time in the Citizen meeting. Later Seb said: 'I've never been more
relieved, it's very satisfying after the silliness of the past couple of
weeks, though I'm still, in a sense, living from day to day. The
risk is not so much injury, but the loss of preparation in May and
June. I would fancy my chance against anyone at either distance
in a one-off, but what I cannot recover this year is the condition I
had for six races in Moscow. Why I'm reasonably confident for
the next six weeks is that, by the time I get to Brisbane, I should
be two seconds faster than tonight over 800 – and when it comes
to the 1,500, that sort of speed is a dominant factor. Whether we
have a world record in Brisbane depends entirely on the shape of
the races. Cram is undoubtedly now the guy to beat, but it will all
depend on that imponderable third lap. Who knows?'

Cram's suggestion a few weeks previously that there was a
myth about the supremacy of Coe and Ovett was an allowable
part of any young athlete's attempt to bolster his own
confidence. He needed to believe he could beat either of them,
and half an hour after Seb's run in Zurich, Cram proved he was
indeed now a man to contend with at 1,500. He followed the
pace-maker through a first lap of almost 57, with Scott and
Maree at the rear of the field. The 800 was passed in 1:54, with
Cram still second, and with 500 metres to go Boit, Walker and
Flynn of Ireland were all at his shoulder. He fended them off
through a last lap not quite fast enough to bring him within reach
of Ovett's world record, but for a time of 3:33.66, the third
fastest of the year. As Seb commented: 'He showed tonight,
perhaps for the first time, the courage to go out in front on his
own with 650 to go. He's three or four years younger than me.
There's been very little this year to choose between those at the
top, and at the moment I guess Cram is at the head of the pile.'
The next few weeks would not see him shifted.

Two

Clouded Silver

By the third week in August it had become evident that Ovett was increasingly unlikely to be able to compete in Athens. Discussion began on whether Seb was fit enough, and could be persuaded to stand in for his rival and run both events, though he himself still had marginal injury problems and might be hard pressed to withstand the stress of six races, never mind three. Ovett had torn a hamstring, was having treatment and could not commit himself to a decision either way, at a time when Seb was winning further races over 800 metres, first at the Talbot Games and two days later in Cologne. He was only briefly bothered in the Talbot Games when Garry Cook, third fastest in the year's ranking, had the chance to overtake him at the end of a mild first lap of 54, coasted behind Belger (USA) and Harrison (GB). But Cook delayed, an Coe prepared for a fast last bend; Guimaraes of Brazil closed the gap but could do no more, and as Seb relaxed down the home straight there was the brief illusion – soon dispelled – that Harrison might catch him. Seb's time was a comfortable 1:45.85.

On he moved to Cologne, where he ran almost a second faster to defeat the Americans Scott and Robinson, and West Germany's hope for Athens, Hans Peter Ferner. Seb burst from the pack with 300 metres to go after a first lap of 52.3, and afterwards said optimistically: 'I feel I can go now to Athens and cope with whatever may happen.' Inconveniently, and ill-advisedly, he was required a week later, along with many of the rest of the British team going to Greece, to attend the Heinz Games at Crystal Palace, where he, Cram, Cook and Peter Elliott made an attempt on the world record for 4x800 metres. It was an appointment none of them relished so close upon a major championship, but one which the Board demanded, in another perverted show of authority to protect the sponsors of a meeting which should never have been arranged at such a time. Seb was still not sure that he would be ready to compete in two events in Athens, or that he would be asked to.

He *was* required to turn up at Crystal Palace. There were three British teams in the attack on the 4x800 record. Peter Elliott, the current AAA champion, gave the first-string squad an unimpressive start with a leg of 1:49.14, well behind Rob Harrison's 1:47.83 for the second team. A crowd of nearly twelve thousand, knowing what was required through announcements from the commentators, began to roar support. Cook caught Steve Caldwell with a second leg of 1:46.20 to put the first team back on schedule, leaving the responsibility on Cram and Coe to do the rest if they could, from out in front. Cram, with 1:44.54, pulled them inside the schedule and now Seb had to maintain it. His scintillating first lap of 49 and the fastest leg of the quartet in 1:44.01, gave Britain the record with 7:03.89, more than four seconds inside the four-year-old mark set by the Soviet Union. 'Seb was standing still when I handed over and I thought he'd decided not to bother!' laughed Cram. It gave Seb a share in his fourth current outdoor world record, but he said: 'Given a choice, I don't think any of us would have been here today. What other national federation would ask their athletes to attempt a world record four days before leaving for a major championship? There were a lot of glum faces in the warm-up area, though in the end I enjoyed it.' It was a sharp answer to any doubting by the Board of individual fitness, though Elliott's return straight from two week's holiday in Spain might have jeopardized the attempt. 'We were the only ones to have to run hard, others went through the motions during the meeting, while we had to put our heads on the block,' said Cram.

When sending the invitations to every athlete who would compete in Athens, the Board attached an ultimatum from John Le Mesurier, secretary to the selection committee, which had stated: 'I have been asked by the council of the Board to point out that all athletes . . . must show their fitness by competing in the

Bank Holiday meeting on 30 August. . . . Those who do not compete will not travel to Athens.'

Nothing could have more clearly shown the breakdown between the Board and the strongest team ever sent to a European Championships, just at a moment when the Board was celebrating its fiftieth anniversary. If sponsors of major fixtures under the Board's administration were not getting value for money because some senior athletes were staying away, neither was the Board showing sensitivity to the individual athletes and their particular requirements. 'It will destroy all goodwill, it takes away our freedom and makes for nothing but bad feeling,' stated Moorcroft, who had been obliged to change the training programme planned by him and his coach, John Anderson. 'I'm not very keen on ultimatums or threats. Co-operation is essential. Don't they understand that the last week before a championship is vital? If the Board had made their demands known earlier, they might have deserved some co-operation.'

A further muddle by the Board became apparent a few days later upon arrival in Athens, when the Greek authorities stated that they had not received Coe's name as a 1,500 metre replacement for the injured Ovett. It seemed the telex was lost; there were anxious communications between Nigel Cooper, the Board secretary, and his staff back in London, all of it portrayed on television as a welcome part of the soap opera before the real action began. Seb himself had hardly had time to consider whether in fact he wished to compete in both events. Eventually the Board's telex was found by a triumphant clerk in London: the first medal of the championships! Discussing his prospects before the 800, at the team's hotel surrounded by sweet-smelling pines in the village of Kifisia, with its clean air high above the summer smog of Athens, Seb said: 'After only five weeks of training since my last injury, I'm living a bit of a charmed life. Every time I race, I'm probably getting a little closer to the limit of my present fitness. Any athlete will tell you that the quicker you are forced to build up your fitness, the more likely you are to hit a sudden trough. So, do I take a chance of running five races here, in two events, or do I hold something back for the Commonwealth Games next month? On the other hand, there is the attraction of two gold medals here, and the measurement of anybody's career is related to the major championships they have won. All I've got is one Olympic title. The complete portfolio must be Olympic, European and Commonwealth medals, and I would like the full set, not to mention the World Championship next year. But by trying for more than one medal here, will I lose out on the Commonwealth because of the limit of my fitness? The emphasis can change. A few weeks ago, failure would have been not getting into the team. Now, failure could be said to be not winning the 800. As for the 1,500, my decision on that must depend on how I get through the next three races of the first event.'

Strange though some might think it, Seb was particularly disappointed that Ovett would be absent from the competition because of injury, giving his time instead to television commentaries. 'We're not particular friends, but my heart goes out to him as an athlete,' said Seb. 'I have a lot of sympathy for him, he must be really depressed. From what I heard about the extent of his thigh injury, it's a surprise he has been able to run at all.' Seb wondered if he himself was going to get to the starting line, when the Opening Ceremony in the beautiful new Athens stadium delayed the start of the first round heats by more than half an hour, and prevented the runners from warming up properly. Seb found himself shut in a room with more than a hundred athletes, not knowing what was happening. First of all the runners were told there was a forty-five-minute delay; then, after some twenty minutes or so, they were instructed to be ready in five minutes.

'I was so tense, I felt as tired at the end of the first lap as I normally do at the end of a race,' said Garry Cook. Seb put the problems behind him, reaching the semi-final with a time of 1:48.46, holding off a challenge from Ferner of West Germany. Cook got through as one of the fastest losers, having finished fourth in his heat. The semi-finals the next day were by no means stringent. In the first, Ferner, with a time of 1:48.71, lead home Druppers (Netherlands), Cook and Wagenknecht (East Germany). In the second, Coe (1:47.98) was never hard pressed by the three other qualifiers behind him: Beyer, the East German winner in 1978, Wulbeck (West Germany) and Harkonen

(Finland). On the face of it, Seb only had to stand up to win the next day. How often has one heard that said before in sport? Back in London, previewing the final for ITV, Ovett voiced the opinion of just about everyone in athletics when he said: 'The rest of them are running for the minor places. Seb has an hypnotic effect on the other runners in any race. They just wait for the moment when he goes.'

For all but 90 metres of the final there seemed to be nothing to challenge Ovett's view. Seb dominated the race. Ferner held the lead at the end of the first back straight, just ahead of Harkonen, the Finnish champion. Then Seb took over, and dictated tactics for the next 400 metres. He went through the bell in 53.24, the sort of pace which should have left him able to toy with any of those in contention. He was relaxed and in control. He led down the third straight and round the final bend, and when the finish came in sight was some two metres clear of the rest of the field, which was led by Ferner and Beyer. Looking at Seb's face, however, from a distance of some 70 or 80 metres, I could sense the anxiety inside him from the way his jaw-line seemed to tighten. There was nothing to spare if anyone came back at him: no possibility of that second or third kick which a year before had been his unanswerable trade mark.

Now, the legs were empty. Half-way down the home straight Ferner, whom he had beaten with ease in Cologne a fortnight before, was coming to his shoulder; was going past him. Seb could not respond, and was beaten to the line by three tenths of a second by a man who had never even won his own national title. Harkonen took the bronze and Cook was fourth.

No one was more astonished than Ovett, whose disbelief reflected the reaction of everyone, not least of the gold and silver medalists themselves. 'I just can't believe it' the three of them all said to different audiences. As Ovett observed, Seb had been in a perfect position throughout the race. 'He probably lost a lot of fitness due to that stress fracture,' said Ovett, searching for an excuse for his rival. Ferner, a twenty-six-year-old physics engineer, seemed as bemused as anyone. 'It's absurd, crazy. I came here only expecting to reach the final.'

For Seb, it was the second stunning reverse in two years, and he struggled in something of a daze to control his disappointment. 'I just cannot understand it, I simply didn't have the legs when it mattered. I've taken too much out of a shallow well,' he muttered. 'I started to wind it up a bit from 300 out, a little bit more from 200, and I got the daylight I needed at about 130 metres out. I guess Ferner passed me at about 40 metres from the line, and I just couldn't hold him off. I didn't do anything wrong or make any errors.'

Peter was grim faced. What he knew, and what as yet had not been disclosed, was that Seb had developed swollen glands. Before the end of the evening Peter had notified the Board that there was no possibility of Seb's competing in the 1,500 metres, and within a day they had withdrawn from the mile in Oregon. Returning straight home for hospital consultation, it was confirmed that Seb had swollen glands and the probability of glandular fever. Whether he might still have had the strength to hang on for victory had he not shared in that recent relay world record would always be open to debate. As soon as his condition was clarified by the hospital, he withdrew from the Commonwealth Games, and was only a television viewer of two masterly tactical victories by Cram for a 1,500 metres double: the gold in Athens with 3:36.49, in front of Kirov (Soviet Union) and Abascal (Spain), and in Brisbane in 3:42.37, ahead of Walker (New Zealand) and Boit (Kenya). The youngster now wore the crown.

Three

Summer of Pain

Spring comes early to the Algarve. Before the end of January, almond blossom lines the narrow roads which wind through the orange groves. The braver of those attending the twelfth congress of the European Athletics Coaches' Association at Acoteias in 1983 had unpacked their shorts, but would return to northern Europe with knees still pallid, for there was no real heat in the sun. The talk in the coffee breaks over the first two days centred on the revelations of two British coaches who, like Charles Atlas, had turned a couple of seven-stone weaklings into world record breakers. Some of the secrets of British middle-distance supremacy were emerging in surroundings about as dramatic as a vicarage jumble sale.

In matter of fact tones Peter Coe and John Anderson had been telling a gathering of 120 international coaches, including the envious East Germans and Russians, how they rewrote coaching theory in the 1970s to convert two spindley schoolboys, Sebastian Coe and Dave Moorcroft, into middle-distance world record holders from 800 metres to 5,000 metres with the most devastating finishing kicks yet seen – when already running at record pace. The key to this factor – Seb ran the last 100 metres of his Moscow 1,500 metres in 12.1 seconds, which is almost respectable 400 metres pace – was the ability of the two athletes to sustain anaerobic running in a middle-distance event. Seb had been the more remarkable in this, but the principle applied equally to Moorcroft, who failed by only a stride to break thirteen minutes for 5,000 metres in Oslo the previous year with his record 13:00.42. Yet the two have approached this pinnacle from opposite directions.

Anaerobic performance is typical of sprinting, where energy is derived from latent power in the muscles and is expended at a rate which quickly leads to an oxygen debt, and the creation of lactic acid which ultimately halts the athlete. Aerobic running, as in the marathon, is dependent on the performer's ability to absorb fresh oxygen into the blood stream, dispersing lactic acid. For distances between the two extremes, the balance between anaerobic and aerobic effort is an imprecise science, but Anderson had said that, long before Seb reached his exceptional upper limits, he knew from the front running characteristics that he must be working on a very high level of anaerobic training.

In 1967 an international seminar on ergonometrics, the study of physiological work capacity, had given the following approximate breakdowns for proportions in the distance ranges, which had provided a yardstick for training schedules for most international coaches:

Distance (metres)	100	200	400	800	1,000	1,500	5,000	10,000
Anaerobic %	95	90	75	55	50	35	10	5
Aerobic %	5	10	25	45	50	65	90	95

Seb was then only eleven and Moorcroft fourteen. Anderson, who became Moorcroft's coach eighteen months later, admits that at that stage he had no conception of Moorcroft's potential, although he feels that if he had not taken over his coaching Moorcroft would have drifted into marathon running in adulthood. Peter, with a father's natural optimism and closer contact, had at the same stage a greater conviction of his young boy's potential, and was convinced his optimum distance would be 1,500 metres. Yet he concentrated from the age of fourteen to seventeen on a twice-weekly winter cross-country programme, to establish the basis of endurance.

Then came Peter's critical decision. Middle-distance running had become obsessed with a work ethic, personified by Dave Bedford: the greater the training mileage, the greater the reward. When Seb was eighteen, Peter had backed off endurance work to concentrate on speed, and especially the ability to sustain speed; with high-quality, intense anaerobic training of severe repetitions over 300, 600 and 800 metres with minimal recovery intervals, and gut-tearing hill work on ten-degree inclines. Simultaneously, Anderson was employing a similar pattern with Moorcroft, the difference being that Coe was naturally a shorter-distance runner who had to produce endurance, while Moorcroft was a longer-distance runner who had to produce speed. In the 1978 European Championships, Coe was on as little as thirty-five miles per week, while Moorcroft and Anderson had already decided, after reaching the Montreal 1,500 metres final two years before, to move up to 5,000 metres in Moscow.

Peter's theory was twofold: when an athlete has reached a certain plateau of endurance capability, additional mileage will produce no further improvement, and the plateau can be maintained on only sixty per cent of the work required to reach it. Two-thirds of the runners in Britain should heed that advice. Secondly, Peter reckoned, the 1967 ergonometric figures were seriously misleading.

For an 800 metres at the pace Seb was now attempting to run, some two seconds or fifteen metres faster than anyone ever before, the proportion between anaerobic and aerobic content was nearer to 70–30 than the 55–45 which had been regarded as standard. His argument was as follows: if Seb ran an 800 metres first lap of 49 seconds compared with a personal best of 46 seconds, then the anaerobic content is likely to be around 65–35. Then, as he put to the congress in Portugal, was the second lap likely to be more or less anaerobic? The deduction was that it had to be *more*, with the subsequent conclusion that the balance for the whole race would be in the region of 70–30. But Peter warned the congress: 'If another coach were to attempt our formula, and get the proportions wrong for that individual, he will destroy his athlete.'

Another problem confronted Peter when Seb was nineteen. Like Moorcroft, his physique was different from the now accepted mould of Snell–Juantorena–Walker. Whilst statistics show that Olympic competitors conform to a 5 feet 11 1/4 inches/11 stone 9 pounds norm for 400 metres, and 5 feet 10 inches/10 stone 5 pounds for 800 metres, Seb was 5 feet 9 1/4 inches/9 stone 4 pounds. If one subtracts from that the weight of skull, viscera and skeleton, there is not much muscle weight for the equation:

force = mass x acceleration. To ensure that Seb had the best possible muscle tone, Peter embarked him on a weight training programme. Within three years, over his time at Loughborough University from 1977 to 1979, Seb was able to reduce his 400 metres time to 45.5 seconds, achieved in the four-lap relay in the Europa Cup Final in Turin. *The alliance of endurance plus unrivalled basic speed had been achieved.* After the set-backs of 1982, Seb and Peter would shortly be re-entering the competitive arena, to put their theories to the test once again, and hoping that any after-effects of glandular fever were now gone.

Seb was due to run 3,000 metres at the national indoor championships at Cosford, and his first appearance since losing in Athens was creating interest amongst the public and athletes. Talking to Dudley Doust of *The Sunday Times* a week before the race he said: 'I'm flattered to hear from what the entries office have told me, that rivals are switching from their event to mine. I'm there to be gunned at and, chances are, I'll get whacked. Fair enough. All I want to do is find out where I am at this early stage of the season. In all, 1982 was one of those years you would like to see the back of. For the first time in a full year, I feel healthy.' In the event, a bad cold suffered during the week obliged Seb to pull out of the race, so that public, media and organizers were left disgruntled; but it was one of those situations in which he would have done himself no favours by competing. He would still be able to show in the coming weeks that his form was encouraging. He agreed to run in the indoor match against France a fortnight later at 1,500 metres, and with a spectacular sprint over the final 200 metre lap he mollified his critics. The instant acceleration, missing in Athens, was back, and that last lap of 25.5 gave him a winning time of 3:42.6.

The sharpness was confirmed four weeks later when he claimed his eleventh world record, and his second indoors; he seemed to stroll through the 800 metres in the match between England and the United States, his time of 1:44.91 shaving more than a second off his record set on the same track two years before. Colin Szwed led through 200, and covered the first two laps in 51; with a lap and a half to go Coe was alone, a familiar situation. Peter Elliott, European indoor silver medallist a week earlier, had run too many hard winter races and was never able to get in touch, and a full house of 3,500 applauded Coe to the line. He was running even faster this March than at the start of 1981, and said afterwards: 'Apart from having flu a month ago I feel happy with the way things are going.' One should not be dismissive about Elliott's performance in second place – only six years back it would have been close to the world record.

Seb, riding his renewed confidence, moved on to another world record eight days later. Competing for England against Norway in Oslo, he took half a second off Peter Wellman's seven-year-old time for 1,000 metres indoors, with 2:18.58. Paced for 600 metres, as the week before, by Szwed of Birchfield, Seb opened out to pass 800 in 1:57.07, and hold on for his fifth record in Norway in as many appearances. Just to show he was in shape, after a week of lecturing and training, he ran the eight miles back to his hotel, with the throw-away line that the race had effectively been 'a training run'. In the way competitors are encouraged to do by appreciative audiences, in the aftermath of success and his twelfth world record, he agreed that it would be nice to achieve a round figure of twenty before he retired!

Changing place, distance and temperature, Seb next appeared publicly in a road race at the little shoe manufacturing town of Vigevano, west of Milan. It was here, three years previously, that he had emerged from an anonymous three months' preparation in Rome for the Olympics; and now, as then, he ran away over the four miles of twisting streets to win in 18:28. It was faster than he had expected. The race had been flag-started by his sister Miranda, who was on holiday in Italy, and it needed half a mile of hard work to get up among the leaders. The first four laps became a duel between Coe and Gelindo Bordin, but over the final lap Coe pulled away to enter the ancient Piazza Ducale, with its stucco terraces, well clear of the young Italian. Back now to native Yorkshire, and his usual track pipe-opener, this time at Cleckheaton, with a slowish 1,500 metres in 3:45. By now he was already beginning to suffer continual abdominal pains which hampered his performances.

At Birmingham in early June, an under-strength British team was overwhelmed by the Soviet Union, yet such is the persistant inability of the Russians to produce middle-distance runners of even average international quality that Seb was able to take the thirtieth Emsley Carr Mile in 4:3.37, the slowest time since Alan Simpson's victory in 1965. Kirov, bronze medallist in the Olympic 800, could finish only third. Just over a week later Seb ran his first outdoor 800 since Athens at the opening of Loughborough's new £200,000 all-weather track, in the annual match against the AAA. His time of 1:44.99 was one-hundredth outside the AAA record he had set three years previously, (which was then on cinders and likely to remain an unofficial world record in such circumstances for many years to come). Peter Elliott, Chris McGeorge, Steve Caldwell and Graham Williamson dominated the running for more than a lap, to cause consternation among the film crew and producers of the company engaged in making a documentary on Seb's running career. He allowed them to breath a little more easily when, 120 metres from home, he fought off the pains which now accompanied any first lap and got going to win by three-fifths of a second from Williamson, whose time of 1:45.6 was a Scottish record. McGeorge was third and Elliott, in his first outdoor defeat of the season, fourth. Seb said afterwards that he had planned a waiting game from the back of the field against his young rivals. If there had been no one in that race who could hurt him yet, there were several coming up who needed to be taken more seriously as opponents even were he at his best.

Indeed, news was filtering through from overseas which suggested that before the end of June he might have to run close to a world record over 1,500 metres in Paris if he were to outstay a twenty-two-year-old Moroccan. Said Aouita had just run the ninth fastest time ever of 3:32.54, best of the year, in Florence, and it was expected that he would be at the Paris Permit Meeting along with various others including José Gonzalez of Spain. This provided Seb with something of a dilemma, for the end of June was earlier than he would have wished to produce any kind of a peak, considering that the World Championships were not until August. Aouita, a former World Student Games champion, had been training at altitude in Mexico, and had achieved his time of just over a second outside Ovett's world record with a last lap of

54, which was faster than any last lap in any world record at 1,500 or a mile. Seb admitted that it might be necessary to run close to 3:31. 'A race at that pace would not be seriously damaging for me at this stage, because in some ways a race is actually easier than training, its like having a couple of days off. If I need to run at that pace I am ready, and it would be encouraging to know I am going well at two distances and also to achieve a qualifying 1,500 metres time for Helsinki.'

Seb was pre-selected by the British Board at 800 metres for the World Championships, but was required to qualify at the longer distance. He knew that his problem, whatever Aouita might be doing, was not to reach a peak too soon – as he did in 1981, when the advent of a serious blister conveniently obliged him to ease off in the three weeks prior to his record breaking duel with Ovett. It is this aspect of the present level of middle-distance running which is virtually unknown to the general public, but which is of constant account to the athlete. 'It's a very humbling sport,' reflected Seb, looking ahead to Paris. 'You are lucky to take out a fraction of what you put in. In a sense, Athens was a good thing for me. Every sportsman needs to be brought up sharp now and then. I'd had three marvellous years since 1979, with some luck in avoiding serious injury, and managing to get away with it when I was slightly injured. It would have been bad, on reflection, for me and for the sport to have come back from Athens with the 800 gold medal after only four weeks of make-shift preparation, having just missed eight weeks with injury. It would have devalued the significance of everything one is doing at a time of normal preparation.' It was strange when one realized that in the last six seasons the world's supreme miler had run no more than fourteen four-lap races, and that one of his reasons for running Paris was actually to remind himself what it was like.

After much speculation in the French press about the prospect of a confrontation between the known and the relatively unknown, Aouita failed to show up at the Jean Bouin stadium, which nestles in the shadow of the Parc des Princes. One of the organizers' solutions for keeping a large crowd happy seemed to be the continuous playing of loud pop music, even while races were in progress. It was not the music which disconcerted Seb.

Forty metres after the gun he was jostled in the pack, caught his foot on the kerb, and tumbled almost headlong into the long jump pit. By the time he had recovered, the rest of the runners were almost twenty metres further on, and it was going to require a stupendous effort to regain this ground, get back among the leaders, and still have any strength left for the finish. Recover he did, and coming into the final straight off the last bend he was neck and neck with Gonzalez. Stride by stride they battled, but Coe could not hold on, and was defeated by three tenths of a second. Deducting between one and two seconds for time lost off the track, never mind the disruption to his rhythm, then Coe's time of 3:35.17 becomes relatively outstanding, and he had only run the distance faster on three occasions. Perhaps the most important lesson to be learned was that he had once again been knocked around when allowing himself to be hemmed in by a bunched field, and this tactical error was something Peter was quick to point out. Tactical frailty in a tough race was a sensitive area which the press were always quick to fasten on to.

Seb had been bundled out of the way in the 1977 Europa Cup Final in Helsinki by Wulbeck of West Germany; was consistently in the wrong place throughout the Moscow 800; and had been boxed in the Moscow 1,500 semi-final. By the time he had gone 40 metres in Paris, he should have been running wide in lane 2, so that going into the first bend he would have space and flexibility both inside and outside. Nonetheless, the cynics were saying that Seb would be able to cry all the way to the bank. This was the first meeting under the new IAAF system of permits, which allowed organizers to pay participation money. The generally reported fee for Seb, following communications between the French and British federations and the IAAF, was £15,000: substantially more than would have been negotiated by the Spaniard who spoilt the climax in the last reel.

Those of us who regularly fly north to Oslo for the summer meetings at Bislett, look forward almost as much to the strawberry party the preceding day, on the sloping lawns under the apple trees at the house of Arne Haukvik, high up in the hills behind the harbour city, as we do to events on the track. In 1983 it was raining. No one could recall such an afront by the weather, but at least it was fine the following evening, and there was the customary calm as the sun went down and the daytime convections quietened. It is difficult to say why such a track, hemmed in by the old streets, and with the smell of the brewery mingling with the embrocation, should be such a mecca. Perhaps it is the history of the place, with the accumulative inspiration of all those previous records. Certainly Seb now found some inspiration four days after his defeat in Paris, recording the third fastest 800 metres of his career in what was much more of a race than a carefully staged record attempt. The field included the current fastest man of the year, Koskei of Kenya, plus Druppers of Holland, Mays of the United States, European indoor champion Trabado of Spain, Elliott and McGeorge. An American, King, set the pace with 51.27 for the first lap, at which speed most of the field was still there with Coe, and several of them were still there approaching the final bend. Coe broke free in the home straight, had time to look over his shoulder once or twice, and recorded 1:43.80, with Elliott getting under 1:45 in third place. The sixth fastest performance ever gave Coe reason to believe that the defeat by Gonzalez was hopefully just a hiccup.

The same evening Ovett, who three days before had dropped out of a race in Edinburgh, removed some of the doubts about him, with the second fastest 1,500 metres of the year, even after being boxed in behind Graham Williamson on the final bend. Ovett forced his way out of trouble coming into the home straight as he barged his way into the second lane occupied by Flynn of Ireland, who lost his balance and sent Abascal head over heels on to his back. Ovett recorded 3:33.81 after overhauling Williamson, who lowered his own best to 3:34.01. Immediately after the race, Ovett admitted to British Independent Television that in a championship he could have been disqualified. Williamson's fine run, however, caused some turmoil within the British Board selection committee, and would also be an embarrassment to Seb – but not as much of an embarrassment as his own next race.

Back home at Crystal Palace for the Talbot Games, he was defeated over 1,500 metres by Dragan Zdravkovic, last in the Moscow final. Seb had taken over the lead after about 1,000 metres from Aldridge, an American, following a fast 800 of around 1:53. Coming into the home straight, Zdravkovic was still at his shoulder and passed him with 50 metres to go. Seb confessed afterwards to being 'mentally shattered', but insisted he would still run the following week in the Invitation Mile at the AAA Championships. What had not become public knowledge at this stage – understandable, since no athlete concedes vital information to his opponents – was that inconsistancies in Seb's training were sufficient to be causing reasonable doubt about his true condition. For some weeks he had suffered stomach pains which restricted his acceleration. It has to be wondered, therefore, whether his decision to continue with the AAA Mile was in any way influenced by financial factors. 'Certainly there were financial considerations,' Seb said. 'But those of Robinson's, the sponsors, more than mine. I didn't want to let them down on a major meeting that had been planned for months.'

The Board selectors were evidently not sure what *they* were influenced by. At a preliminary meeting to consider the four candidates for 1,500 metres in the World Championships – Cram, Ovett, Williamson and Coe – the first three were initially nominated, presumably with deference to Williamson's performance in Oslo. The Board were confused, not only about the respective merits of individuals, but about the principle of allowing any athlete, notably Coe and Ovett, to double up. Through an unintended leak to a news agency, it became known that Williamson and Cram had been deleted from an original selection, presumably in deference to the Olympic Champion. This now meant that Williamson, who had better 1,500 times for the season than Cram and Coe, might be obliged to run off for the final place with Cram, if Coe were to produce world record form in the AAA Mile – to which neither Cram nor Williamson were invited.

The difficulty for the selectors was that Cram, European and Commonwealth champion, had suffered a season disrupted by injuries and, privately, did not expect to be chosen. Williamson, however, having one of his best seasons after a chapter of misfortunes over the years, was agrieved at the selectors' oscillation and considered, moreover, that they were jeopardizing his prospects should they ultimately choose him. He said, too, and not without some justification, that preferential treatment was being given to Coe.

Seb, with more than enough problems of his own without being the public pig-in-the-middle of a controversy that was not of his making, decided to resolve the issue unilaterally. Four days before the AAA Mile, he formally withdrew his wish to be considered for the longer distance, and gave a statement to the domestic news agencies in which he claimed that he had been placed in an untenable position. The three main points of his protest were: one, the public debate by the selectors, with their comments to the press, had presented a one-sided picture; two, the impression created in the press that he was receiving special consideration at the expense of others; and three, the Board should have decided upon a head-to-head selection race, which he had always advocated, rather than arguing over the relative merits of individual performances in different races, among which his were not the slowest.

It was, of course, not appropriate for him to say so, but if the Board were giving him special consideration, then that is the proper right of an Olympic champion. The point that he was at pains to make was that if he were now selected, it would put him under pressure from the outset. If he did anything less than gain a medal, it would be claimed that someone else should have been selected. He stressed that five weeks previously he had urged the Board not to delay selection. 'I was willing to meet anyone head-to-head, and considered I was the one being avoided by the others,' he said. Peter was an approving party to the statement, because he considered his son had been the innocent victim of the controversy. Nigel Cooper, secretary to the Board, professed to be amazed at Coe's decision, while the final twist was that on the same day that Seb told Frank Dick, the national coach, that he was withdrawing from consideration, Cram and Williamson had been told by Andy Norman, one of the selectors, that they had an open invitation to run in the AAA Mile. It was a tale from which no official could emerge with dignity.

It would be facile to say, with hindsight, that Seb and Peter might have been motivated in their decision by their inside knowledge of Seb's physical problems, of which the defeat in the Talbot Games by Zdravkovic was only part of the evidence. Why not, it could have been argued, withdraw from one event in Helsinki in order to concentrate on the other, under the camouflage of the controversy? But that would be to deny the fundamental integrity of Seb, in whom I personally believe. By coincidence, I was scheduled that week to write a profile of him in *The Times* and, inevitably, the controversy was one of the aspects of his overall ambitions for the World Championships which I had discussed with him. There was no doubt, whatever his physical condition, that when he woke up that week to read headlines such as 'Coe Reprieved' (*Daily Mail*) and 'Selectors Accused of Bias' (*The Times*), he decided his reputation took precedence over his ambition – however strong his ambition might be to achieve in Helsinki the double which had eluded him Moscow. As he said, having surprised both officials and public by his decision: 'If I had not considered I was capable of running better than all the other contenders for the 1,500, I would have pulled out earlier. It is a fact which most officials and journalists do not understnad, that athletes performing at my level set higher standards for themselves than anybody else. I have been put in an impossible position by the public debate, by the impression that I was receiving favours.'

What must always be considered with Seb is his mental resilience under pressure, epitomized by his recovery from defeat in Moscow. To suggest that his withdrawal now was a cop-out, following two defeats, was to misunderstand the man. What would later become apparent to me was that Peter and Seb were both almost *refusing* to contemplate a reduction of their ambitions, in spite of the esoteric evidence that perhaps they should; and that the stronger force in this determination was the son's. Of course he was hurt by those defeats. The only protection for the super-star from the ferocious pressure of being continually under the public microscope – something of which Williamson and Cram as yet knew almost nothing compared to Ovett and Coe – is the carapace of continual victory. Defeated, the champion is as vulnerable and disregarded as the leader of the

Cook, Cram, Elliott and Coe at Crystal Palace in August celebrate the
4x800m world record of 1982 – which they would rather not have run
(Associated Press Ltd)

Hans–Peter Ferner of West Germany can hardly believe his European
triumph in Athens. Coe was second and Haerkoenen of Finland (120) third
(Popperfoto)

Jogging with his friend Irene Epple, the West German Olympic skier. The conflict of their competitive seasons restricted their time together *(Express Newspapers)*

The inescapable truth: the 1983 defeat at Gateshead, fourth behind Cram (6), Wuycke of Venezuela (4) and Elliott (7), which told Coe he was ill *(Neville Pyne)*

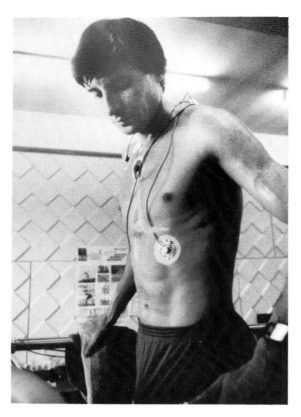

Prolonged study, using a
running treadmill (left) and
oxygen–intake analysis
(below) at Loughborough
University's physiology
laboratory, confirms that
Seb's recovery is satisfactory.
Peter Coe (left) and Clyde
Williams, lecturer at the
University's department of
Physical Education, monitor
the apparatus
*(Both photos: Hugh Hastings/
Creative Communications)*

Right: Seb gives a lift to Garry Ward, one of his pace-making colleagues at the Haringey Club, on the snow-covered slopes surrounding New River Stadium, where he did much of his work to regain peak fitness. *Below:* Some hard work on Richmond Hill, with the Thames in the background, soon after he had started to run again
(Both photos: Hugh Hastings/ Creative Communications)

Footwork avoiding the deer in Richmond Park (above) can be simpler than it occasionally is on the track, where Coe is jostled from behind by Graham Williamson (57) (left), and nearly goes down in a controversial AAA 1,500m final in June 1984. Peter Elliott is the eventual winner, obscured just behind Williamson
(*Top: Ian Stewart/Times. Left: Popperfoto*)

A late burst by Elliott in the final few yards gives him victory over Coe in the AAA 1,500m final – a result which sparked press and public demand for Elliott to be preferred for the remaining place in the Olympic team *(Popperfoto)*

Seb and his father in the Los Angeles Olympic village on one of the few occasions
they saw each other between the defeat in the AAA Championships and the
Olympic victory. For practical reasons, they had agreed to limit their tactical
discussions to regular talks on the phone prior to, and during, the Games. Peter
stayed with friends at Long Beach during the races, but their collaboration remained
as intimate as ever *(Ian Stewart/Times)*

wolf pack. On the track no less than in front of the footlights, you are only as good as your last performance.

Seb had openly faced the press in defeat, and after the Talbot Games had himself projected the possibility of exclusion from Helsinki by the selectors for the 1,500 metres. He had never sought to introduce into the selectors' consideration the mitigating factors of his stomach strain, or the ankle injured when jumping out of the way of a dog in training. Yet it was on these counter-balancing factors that the Coes themselves were still estimating that a bid for both titles was not only justified but realistic. As one of the selection committee had said to me: if either Coe or Ovett were capable of doubling up, it would be irresponsible not to allow it. It needed to be recognized that Seb's ambition was not merely to win selection, but to win the championship. Yet even before the selection fiasco, Coe had stated: 'Whatever I feel about the selectors' ultimate decision is unimportant. I have to accept it if I am excluded, and not waste mental energy questioning it, though I would have to look at the result in Helsinki afterwards and ask if they had been correct.'

The muddle at the initial selection meeting, with general secretary Nigel Cooper involved in the premature announcement and subsequent withdrawal, may have been inefficient, but as one of the selectors told me: 'I believed Coe is capable of running both events, but we debated whether it was our duty to protect athletes from their own ambitions in world championships where the standards and pressures will be enormous.' The selectors were truly as vulnerable as the competitors, but what had most hurt Seb's pride was that seemingly not one of the eight selectors was initially prepared to back him for a place in both races. 'The bottom line was that none of them considered I was certain to finish in front of any of the other three.'

Prior to the AAA Mile, at least, Seb was still entitled to be offended by such a stance. An innovation of that mile was that for the first time in 103 years the AAA would be prepared to compromise with tradition, dispense with qualifying heats, and stage the race in late evening for the benefit of American television viewers. It was another evening of dismay for Seb, in

spite of the satisfaction of defeating Williamson. Although
running another well-judged tactical race, and always being in a
perfect position to strike at any time in the last lap, he was unable
to respond to the early kick of the twenty-six-year-old American
Steve Scott, who won by almost ten yards in 3:51.56. 'My
acceleration is missing, and I don't know why,' Seb said
afterwards. 'I did everything right, but when I pressed the
accelerator there was nothing there. I'm mystified. But I will
continue preparing for the 800 in Helsinki.'

Ovett, injured in the AAA 800 final the next day, was also
denied the opportunity to double up in Helsinki, in spite of his
reasonably fast time in the heats. Thus the selectors' final choice
was Coe, Cook and Elliott for the 800 metres, and Cram,
Williamson and, if fit, Ovett for the 1,500 metres. The modest
and always rational Scott had put his finger on things when he
said after his victory that he doubted if Seb was fully fit. The
inescapable proof of that was about to be delivered.

Competing a week later in the Rank Xerox Games at
Gateshead, Seb was beaten not only by Cram, but into fourth
place by Wuyke of Venezuela and Elliott, all of whom swept past
him on the run-in, in a less than spectacular time, Cram winning
with 1:45.03. Seb was distraught, as might be expected. There
was no hiding from this ultimate exposure of his alarming
decline so close to the World Championships. Several journalists
attempted to speak with the fallen hero, as he pulled on his track
suit and stared unbelievingly into empty space, his world in
shreds. Peter, with a gesture of protectiveness, thrust a pair of
shoes in front of Seb's face, as though to embargo his reactions. It
was an action which would come to be grossly misinterpreted in
the days ahead.

The game was up. Seb and Peter were finally confronted with
the truth they could not avoid. He was ill. The next day he went
back to hospital in Leicester, where he had been after the defeat in
Athens a year before, and was immediately instructed to scratch
from Helsinki. The Board attempted in vain to gain permission
for a late replacement.

Within twenty-four hours the hospital had removed one of the
swollen glands from beneath Seb's left arm, and conducted a

biopsy to ascertain what precisely was wrong. Bracing himself against the collapse of his ambition to win a major 800-metre championship, and the disintegration for the second time in twelve months of two years' dedicated work since the record-breaking spree of 1981, Seb knew that he had to discover an answer to the medical question: was he running badly because he was ill, or was he ill because he ran too much? Only when he had been given a satisfactory answer would he be able to decide whether he would again subject his body to the endlessly rigorous demands of a world class athlete's training, and whether he would continue in the sport he had dominated for the past four years through to the next Olympics.

Seb told me: 'I'm only a year away, optimistically, from another Olympic final. I have to get to the bottom of this, if I'm ever to run seriously again. It seems that something is working through my system related to stress. I need the doctors to tell me why. If they can, then hopefully my future is OK. But if not, there is no way I'm again going to give six solid months of my life to running, free of every other consideration, and then find myself on the wrong end of the life-cycle of a virus on some particular day in Los Angeles, just when I need to be at a peak. I have got to know before I commit myself again that I can get through a whole season intact.'

Endocrinology as yet has produced no certain knowledge of the effect upon the human glandular system of the enormous stresses, muscular and chemical, created by the training schedules over many years of a runner such as Coe, Ovett or Cram. It would be almost preferable for Seb to discover that he *did* have some condition or disease, providing it was cureable, that was unrelated to any self-imposed stress. Yet the suspicion that he might have leukaemia was deeply alarming. Cause and effect remained to be diagnosed while he endured the infinitely depressing physical and emotional withdrawal from his immediate objective. His only consolation was that the critics, who had been less than subtly suggesting that he had forgotten how to win, now had a more rational explanation for his failures. When he lost three races in Paris and London, even Seb and Peter could persuade themselves to argue that he might still turn the corner, though deep down they knew that all was not as it should be. A runner of his standard spends so much of every year, especially during the peak training period some two months before a championship, feeling so tired that he can hardly climb the stairs, that it is difficult for him to know whether he is feeling 'normal' or actually unwell. But that Sunday, when he ran a perfectly judged 800 metres and made his familiar attack on the final bend, only to finish fourth and looking as if he were running in soft sand, the full force of his private nightmare could no longer be ignored. As in Athens a year before, his body had again lost the ability to produce past extravagances. 'Of course it hurts when younger runners like Elliott are suddenly going past you, and on Sunday I knew that all arguments about tactics were now empty. Two weeks ago I began to wonder about my condition. My preparation had not been all it should have been because of the stomach strain, and I decided with Peter to cut right back on training, just to keep sharp and fast, because in comparison with past experience I was feeling more tired than I should have been.'

A record 14,000 crowd had cheered Cram to victory, but in reality it had been sad day for British athletics. There had been no crowing from the young winner, whose instinct told him the score for the loser.

Four

Added Insult

If some of the press and public had not been so fickle towards Sebastian Coe, I might never have been writing this story. Nonsense? Perhaps not. There is no doubt in my mind, nor in Seb's, that some of the criticism of his misfortune and failures between 1982 and 1984 at least in part helped to give him that determination to recover, to demonstrate to those who too quickly wrote him off that they were wrong. There is a belligerence in him which is rarely seen in public, a totally camouflaged bloody-mindedness in his running, which is all part of his exceptional will-power. As one of his closest friends says: 'There are some sensitive parts of him which run deep, but so deep that most people never see them, or are aware that they are there.' It is a strange blend of serenity and mental aggression which he inherits not from his father Peter but from his mother's side of the family. There are those who know the family who might mischievously say that it is only that serenity which has enabled Angela, Seb and the other three children to tolerate, often with humour, Peter's sometimes excitable and pedantic preoccupation with detail. Yet Peter's patience, on the other hand, allied to his clinical eye for detail, are equally a part of Seb's achievements. If inheritance moulds our characters as much as environment does, Seb has cause to be grateful for his inheritance.

I am, of course, on thin ice when discussing the behaviour of the press. Dog does not eat dog. Nevertheless, we should all be able to stand back and look objectively at our colleagues. Having worked during the past twenty-eight years for five newspapers, for periods of not less than two years each – *The Times*, *Daily Telegraph*, *Sunday Telegraph*, *Daily Express* and then *The Times*

53

again – one sees both vices and virtues. The relationship between sportswriters and competitors is often subjective, on both sides. Sportsmen, the writer soon learns, have an infinite capacity to absorb praise, but all too quickly resent anything even slightly critical. It is part of the sportsman's psychology to rationalize his bad performances, to the point where they are not his fault. If he could not cast off misgivings about the bad days, he could never raise the morale to go out again the next day.

However hard they may try not to be, sportswriters can be equally subjective. What the competitor and the official too often overlook is that the enthusiastic writer is often almost as keen for a patriotic success as the performer, and is moved by the advent of failure to allow his own disappointment to colour his writing accordingly. The honest writer would always far rather cover a success story than a failure, and it must be admitted that success is a boost to the sale of papers. There is therefore no immediately apparent advantage to be had from undue criticism, unless of course the writer can see that criticism might help induce some change for the better. So why should it have been that some of the public and certain journalists tended to like Sebastian Coe rather less as his success continued, and to dismiss him, with a lack of affection, when events turned against him?

What is difficult to understand is the British tendency to knock some of our sporting heroes when they get to the top and stay there, as if their continued prominence somehow makes us feel uncomfortable. Certainly we demand that our heroes be modest rather than arrogant, which begs the question of whether it is actually necessary to be arrogant to get to the top. We also have a tradition, which we may soon have to adjust, by which we do not like our sportsmen to be too rich, at least not ostentatiously so. No one could be less ostentatious off the track than Seb, yet the temperature of his popularity moved inversely, I suspect, to talk of his receiving tens of thousands of dollars every time he ran. We like our heroes to be self-effacing, like Henry Cooper or Bobby Charlton. I think we would approve of Carl Lewis even less than the Americans do. The British public like to think that their sporting heroes or heroines *need* their loyalty. When Seb won in Los Angeles, the public was happier for him once again, because he had become the *underdog* in the months before. The mood of the journalists was more difficult to discern. They had to admire him for a stupendous performance: but did they have any affection for him again? Maybe not. He had proved he could win without their patronage, that the nice guy he had seemed all those years concealed a hard interior.

Seb fits no sporting stereotype. He is one of few in recent years to emerge from a middle-class background and reach the top, articulate enough for the press not to be patronizing, friendly enough for them not to be offended. For six years until 1982, he had given every interview any journalist had ever asked for. He was the journalist's dream: successful, photogenic, coherent. And modest. If there was a nettle, it was occasionally the tetchiness of Peter, who was happy to be regarded as an authority, but not as a commodity. He tended to have the same attitude towards journalists as hospital matrons or magistrates do: 'keep your questions to the point.' When Seb finally crumbled in 1983, Peter's paternal concern was bound to take precedence over considerations for the press, and he regarded them, as might many a parent in a comparable situation, as an intrusion. In relations with the Coes, the press has always had the problem of dealing with two totally differing personalities.

Part of the responsibility of the press in a free and democratic country is to be constantly asking the right questions. Therefore when Seb failed, just as when Alf Ramsey or Dave Bedford or David Gower failed, the inevitable reaction was to be asking, why? In August 1983, the *Daily Mail*, with instant tabloid professionalism, asked the question, but a shade too swiftly. Two days after Seb's disintegration at Gateshead, they published an analysis of alleged facts which they considered could be going wrong. Unfortunately, the article was probably written and ready to appear when it was learned from hospital that Seb had a glandular infection; and a sixth paragraph seemed hurriedly to have been inserted in the story to cover the writer, given the by-line Derrick Young – someone who, if he knew athletics, had seldom been read on the subject previously. Did he really exist at all, or was it a desk job?

The article listed six factors which might individually or

collectively be at the root of Seb's failure: ill-health; psychology; commercialism; family breakdown; over-training; and public pressure. It was the comments on his relationship with his father which were the most offensive to Seb, at a time when he knew that his collapse was exclusively medical. The *Mail* article alleged that Peter drove his son too hard as a boy, put too great an emphasis on success, and deliberately increased the pressure on both of them; that there had been disagreements between them during the summer; that they were growing apart and that Seb was now looking after his own training. Little of this would stand up to serious examination by anyone knowing the true facts. The article also contained allegations from Alan Pascoe, former Olympic competitor, that Seb's problem was mental: that he was over-trained and too involved in commerce. The writer ambivalently intended well, because he concluded: 'Perhaps we could all adjust our attitudes and give him a helping hand.' It could be said that the helping hand of the *Mail* would enormously lift his motivation, if for no other reason than to prove the paper wrong. If nothing else, the article was an embarrassment to Ian Wooldridge and Brian James, two of the paper's leading feature writers, whose long-standing friendliness with Seb was forfeited by such inaccuracies.

Shortly before the Los Angeles Games, discussing his prospects in *Going for Gold*, an ITV publication edited by Richard Russell (and whose contributors included Alan Pascoe), Seb said:

Despite the fact that I wasn't either in perfect health or fully fit, certain journalists, whom I had previously trusted and made myself available to, opted to knock me, without ever bothering to check why I wasn't running as they, and I, wanted me to. Some even accused me of ducking confrontation with other athletes. My answer then, as it is now, is that if it was true, why on earth did I elect to run that 800 metres at Gateshead. As many people know, the crowd there is always knowledgeable and highly partisan, never more so than when Steve Cram is racing. Despite my poor form, and in the knowledge that Cram, Wuyke, Elliott and Cook were competing, I still elected to run. Was that the attitude of a shirker? There is no doubt that such unnecessary and inaccurate journalism has changed my attitude to the press considerably. In future I will find it extremely difficult to convince myself that I should go up to the press box in the way I used to.

The doubts and accusations were by no means confined to journalists. Within the space of the next few months Seb would be written off by Dave Bedford, John Walker and a number of other athletes and coaches who began to feed on the general impression that he was somehow over-trained. Most prominent sportsmen, if they have any maturity, can accept from other competitors an opinion that they are in decline, if it is true – however disappointing this may be. But to be dismissed out of hand when you are ill is particularly stinging. Bedford was quoted as commenting: 'It breaks my heart to say it, but I think Seb is finished.' Even more hard to swallow was the obituary from Walker, who stated: 'The party's over. Great athletes get perhaps two years when they can do almost anything. Seb was maybe the finest middle-distance runner I have ever seen. But he's had his two years.'

When I arrived in Helsinki for the World Championships, a flood of speculation was taking place about the reasons for Seb's absence, all ignoring the real one. One of the allegations rife in Finland was that he had broken down because of the stimulant drugs he was supposedly taking, while coaches such as John Allen made random speculation on deficiencies in his training. As Seb would say later in an interview with *Woman's Realm*, it was sad how fickle the public and press could be.

People used to tell me how the press builds you up and knocks you down, and I didn't want to believe it, probably because in the early years the press was on my side. Throughout the whole build up with Ovett, I was Mr Nice Guy. But now I've come to realize that the pendulum soon swings the other way. I know that recognition in the streets is a small price to pay for all the fantastic support I have had from the public, but it can be a bit hard on friends and family. If the press can't find you for a quote, then they track down someone who knows you. Recently a Sunday paper tried to track a friend of mine when he was on his honeymoon in Tenerife. The other day some photographers went across to our neighbours and asked if they could take some pictures from the bathroom window. It's very difficult to have a private life. I've got used to it now but for friends and family it can be unnerving. It's always difficult with girl friends. You know that any relationship, serious or otherwise, will sooner or later end up in some newspaper.

And in another interview, concerning his friendship with Irene Epple, who had been pursued over the mountains by newsmen:

She couldn't believe what was happening to her. We had been together just three times. Then this. No wonder in her next race she finished sixteenth. As a fellow competitor I know how much she would resent this effect upon her performance. I would be mad to expect any girl permanently to share the present life that has to be so self-regarding . . . training and running coming first . . . university life a close second . . . and socializing coming nowhere.

Perhaps the oddest article of all during the winter of 1983–84 appeared in the *Daily Star*, beside the blurb 'Another STAR exclusive'. It was a strangely exclusive article, considering that Seb had told the writer, who never normally covers athletics, that he was sorry but there was absolutely nothing whatever that he wished to say to him about his recovery or hopes for the Olympics. The writer duly came up with an article saying that Seb was 'as approachable as Frank Sinatra on a bad night' and that he was 'a tormented athlete who knew the game may be up'. What puzzled Seb was to know whether it was an exclusive revelation that he wasn't prepared to speak, or whether the *Star* made a habit of denegrating those sportsmen who were alleged to have spoken to them exclusively.

They were hard months for him. He deliberately avoided being exposed to the coverage of the World Championships by going on holiday to Italy with the friend, a teacher, with whom he shares a house in Loughborough – though in Italy they could not escape from the celebrations of Cova's 10,000 metres victory. It was going to take Seb many weeks to get back to anywhere near normal.

'When you are only 9 stone 4 pounds, and your clothes start hanging off you, and close personal friends are looking at you because they know you are unwell, it's unnerving,' he recalled. 'I have to be grateful to Karl Nicholson, the specialist at Leicester. He was on a hiding to nothing, medically, if he failed to find a cure, and the prospects of that were by no means one hundred per cent. I was a bit chilled, after Gateshead, when he said that not only would I not be going to the World Championships, but he wanted me back in as soon as they had a bed in a ward. The next day another surgeon, who was going to do the biopsy on the gland under my arm, was prodding around saying 'we've got a real juicy one here'. Some fairly unpleasant things go through your mind. Three or four days later they called me at home, having removed the gland, to say they thought they'd 'cracked' it. For the next six or eight weeks I was taking tablets which made me feel terrible.

'The idea of maybe never running again was less overriding than the wish simply to feel *well* again. I hadn't felt well for a year and a half. In addition to being ill following Athens, I had a lot of pain from my back and stomach. Even getting in and out of a car sometimes hurt. For much of the 1983 racing season I was on pain-killers. Mechanically, I literally couldn't *move* properly. So actually stopping running was in some ways a relief. I didn't become *sure* that I could run again until March or April 1984. The proof was not going to be in endurance, but in track work. The other winter work had to be done, but I wouldn't begin to know the truth until I got out on the track. By April I was feeling quite refreshed after each training session, I wasn't falling asleep all the time as I had been in 1983. Once, in Sheffield, going back home for a coffee after training with Peter, I fell asleep in the time it took him to boil the kettle, I was regularly having to stop at service centres on the M1 between Loughborough and Sheffield because my eyes would start closing, and the same on the way to London. I'd pull in at Newport Pagnell for ten minutes, and wake up an hour and a half later.'

It should be mentioned here what Seb had missed in Helsinki. Willi Wulbeck, the twenty-eight-year-old West German, ran what could be called the race of his life to win an 800 metres which would be recalled by the British for a courageous run into fourth place by young Elliott. There were four men in the final who had run faster than Wulbeck that year, and two – Robinson of America and Cruz of Brazil – who were substantially faster than his best ever. Yet with a determined, ungainly surge off the last bend, Wulbeck came from behind to record 1:43.65, a whole second faster than he had previously run, way back in 1979. The favourite, Cruz, was pipped on the line by Druppers of Holland, as the strength faded from the gallant Elliott over the last 20 metres. His brave performance nonetheless gained him a personal best of 1:44.87, and one could not ask more than that.

One of the upsets had occurred in the heats, when the former world record holder Juantorena, now thirty-two, tripped over the kerb at the finish of his race for what should have been an easy passage into the semi-finals, tore his ankle, and instead ended in hospital. It was a sad anti-climax for another great competitor who had been running his fastest for six years. Others who failed to reach the final were the three Kenyans, Ndiwa, Maina and Koskei, and Cook. As the finalists set off, Elliott was on the inside lane and hard on the heels of Cruz just outside him. As they came off the lane-break, Elliott was still pushing at Cruz's shoulder and the two youngest men in the race, both twenty, were leading by three yards from the European champion, Ferner, with Wulbeck and Druppers holding as they rounded the second bend. At the bell these five were grouped close, with Elliott having taken over the lead in 50.6. It had always been the intention of the youngster from Rotherham to try and make it a hard first lap, however much that might be helping those behind him with stamina rather than finishing speed. Round the third bend and into the back straight he held his own, Cruz edging ahead by 600 but with Elliott having visions of a medal. Twice Cruz tried to kick out but could not throw him off. Wulbeck now started to make his effort from third place, towing Druppers with him. With 70 metres to go Wulbeck was level with Cruz and Elliott and steadily gaining. Forty metres out Elliott was still there with a chance of a medal, but Druppers, who would be annoyed that he still had some running left in him at the line, had the speed to take him past two men for the silver with 1:44.20. Wulbeck had become the fifth fastest man ever (with a German record) behind Coe, Juantorena, Wohlhuter and Boit.

The 1,500 metres provided a fascinating canvas. Could Cram and Ovett take two of the medals from a final in which, as Cram suggested, any of the nine runners might reasonably believe he had a chance? Cram's confidence had been increased by his Gateshead win over Seb, though reflecting on his earlier problems he had said before the start of the heats: 'I think my main concern is the question of three races in the three days, especially what is likely to be a really hard semi-final, and I'll have a better idea of the final when I see how I come out of the semi.' He might be European and Commonwealth champion but he remained modest and objective, and refused to accept the suggestion that Scott could not take the pressure of a major championship, pointing out that he had yet to run in one. Cram knew, too, that Aouita had to be taken seriously because of his finishing speed. My view was that Cram ought to win, that Scott's strength would get him the silver, and that Ovett, against a recent background of breakdowns over two laps, would be edged out of the bronze by one of the Africans or Maree. I should have placed a bet. After precisely that had happened, I was informed by a colleague that the odds with a bookmaker would have been 400 to 1 for the first four in order!

In the event, Maree failed to make the final, as did Williamson, with a foot injury, Flynn and Byers. There were six in the line-up who had previously gone under 3:34, yet the first lap of 65 was slower than that of Mary Decker in the women's event. The essential part of Cram's strategy was derived from the knowledge, acquired through something overheard by Brendan Foster, that Aouita intended to make his break 500 metres from the finish: which was exactly what he did, and Cram was ready. Ovett in the early stages looked comfortable, as indeed he should at such an easy pace. It was not until the fourth bend that Cram began to move out from sixth position, Aouita going with him, and down the second last back straight they had closed in behind the front three, Kubista (Czechoslovakia), Zdravkovic (Yugoslavia) and Becker (West Germany). Coming up to the bell the order was changing radically: Aouita shot through on the inside to lead from Cram, Scott and Abascal, with Ovett boxed in, eighth, behind the previous leaders, anxiously searching for a way through. There was none. At no time in any of his major victories between 1977 and 1981 had Ovett ever been more than two or three yards off the leading pace; that he was so far off now suggested as much a physical as a mental problem, though he would say later that he 'just ran badly' – and he still had enough left in him to run a new world record before the season was out.

Down the last back straight Aouita was doing all he could to throw off Cram, without success: his third 400 took only 54.8. Cram remained comfortable at the little Moroccan's shoulder, and went past him going into the final bend. It was here, still some way adrift, that Ovett clashed with Kubista as he battled to get back into contention. He could do no better than take fourth behind Aouita, whose strength faded in the last 50 metres, allowing Scott to get in for the silver by a yard or so. Cram's time of 3:41.59 told clearly enough the story of the early part of the race. 'With 200 to go I sensed no one was in direct contact behind me so I made my effort,' he said. 'I expected them to come back at me but they didn't. I hope it's not the end of an era – Steve Ovett was not at his best. Yet only eight weeks ago I myself had thought that '83 would be a disaster for me.'

It had been an odd sort of first World Championships, with too many slow and cautiously tactical races. At the official reception on the final evening, the promotors of the Permit Meetings from around the world moved in stealthily to arrange what they regarded as the real business of the next month: sharp-eyed, smooth tongued and their pockets metaphorically bulging, while negro athletes swayed to the bossa nova, showing off to the flaxen Nordic girls by simultaneously balancing full beer-glasses on their heads. The Scandinavians bopped up and down self-consciously like Ted Heath's shoulders, and the heavy men from the throws stood around sphynx-like, their pint mugs seeming no bigger than egg-cups in those bucket hands. It was like the Newmarket sales. 'Now I'm trying to arrange some *proper* races,' said Arne Haukvik with a mischievous smile. The question was: what was any longer real? Some of the cat-and-mouse races we had seen, between stars competing not to achieve athletic excellence but for the prestige of medal positions which would subsequently enhance their market value on the

international circus where record breaking attemps are bought
and sold, were no less real than those staged, carefully
choreographed races which were now being negotiated.

One of the world records that autumn would be Ovett's, at
Rieti near Rome in September, when he grabbed back the 1,500-
metre record claimed by Maree the previous week in Cologne,
with 3:30.77 against Maree's 3:31.24. That achievement
persuaded Ovett to agree to race again with Cram, at the IAC-
Coca-Cola meeting, over a mile, won by Cram in a scintillating
finish with 3:52.56 by a stride and a half. After this splendid close
to the domestic season, the two Britons talked to the press about
selection for the Olympics the following year, and whether
Britain, having the world record holder, the world champion
and the Olympic champion (Seb), could expect to take a clean
sweep of the medals. Neither of them thought this was likely,
but both stressed that the controversies of the past summer had
done nothing to help the athletes.

Of course, athletes will always claim that, once they have
established themselves, they should be given a cotton-wool path
to the major championships and not be obliged to leave some of
their best running on minor tracks in a cut-throat procedure to
requalify themselves; that outstanding results in one season
should maintain credibility with the selectors at least until the
next, provided the athletes could demonstrate they were fit.
Cram:

> We've got a much better chance of arriving in a good condition in
> Los Angeles if we're allowed to prepare in our own way, and don't
> have to satisfy the selectors all the time. The fiasco this season is
> something that is not only bad for us and for the selectors, but bad for
> the sport. We make far more important decisions for ourselves.
> We've got to get ourselves in the right condition for Los Angeles,
> and we are in a much better position to do that than the selectors are,
> and if either of us thought we weren't fit enough to go and do well,
> we just wouldn't go. We wouldn't be stupid enough to go unfit.
> We're sensible enough to think for ourselves.

This belief would be called into question, and the perennial
doubts of the selectors in part justified, by the health problems

with which Ovett set off for Los Angeles in 1984, where he ran into such misfortune. It would certainly be right that Seb should have to demonstrate his unquestioned fitness after the reversals of two summers – yet that would lead to further controversy all round.

The selectors are not all stupid, and some of them do try to achieve an intelligent understanding of the finely balanced physical and personal idiosyncracies which can separate an athlete from success and failure over a period of even a few days in the middle of a racing programme – the more so, the better the athlete. It is perhaps worth illustrating some of these issues by reproducing here a couple of items from *Athletics Weekly*, the specialist magazine edited by Mel Watman, which reveal the sort of subtleties and sensibilities that exist between an athlete and his coach, and are mostly an unknown area for nearly all the public and some of the press who seek to pass judgement upon their actions. The first is from an interview with Peter Coe given to Tony Ward, chairman of the British Milers' Club, in the autumn of 1982, taped and transcribed by Dave Cocksedge; and the other a letter from Peter to *Athletics Weekly*, previously reproduced in *Running Free*, a book I wrote with Seb in 1980.

Talking to Tony Ward:

On Peter's cycling background: It had a positive and a negative effect. It taught me that you can push yourself at hard effort for a long way and the damage it is claimed you are doing is not in fact all that serious. I also realized that Seb had all the talent that I lacked and this helped through some hard years. There was no technical advice available locally that was of any value. I used to listen to the trackside sages and quickly realized that all their advice was contradictory. That was one of the better reasons I signed Seb up with the BMC in 1970. I was looking for better information; better coaching/training advice and material that would hang together, make sense to me and stand up to analysis.

On his decision to coach Seb himself: It was not arrogance, or a desire to get more knowledgeable than anyone else. I've always had a semi-romantic notion about the renaissance man; the complete physical and intellectual male human being. What goes on between your ears is as important as what goes into your legs and lungs in training terms. I felt I was in the best position (if I could devote enough time to it) to develop him as a whole person. If you can avoid the pitfalls of getting emotionally involved with your own son, you have the advantage of being able to know more about him, as an individual, than anyone else. It's a full-time job, but you see him in every environment, how he reacts in all areas of his development. You don't just see him training and racing. I don't want to sound like a cheap Penguin book on Psychology, but a parent does get a better insight into a son/daughter than anyone else. If you can ally that to specific knowledge, real knowledge relating to running, you are in a very strong position.

Avoiding the pitfalls: It's all to do with good management. My life is spent managing a business and getting things done in a manufacturing concern, and here you learn techniques of being businesslike and dispassionate although you are dealing with people. I resort to mental tricks, referring to Seb as 'my athlete' rather than 'my son'. Little tricks like that manage to distance you from too much emotional involvement. The danger with only one athlete is that success or failure tends to take on an extra-large dimension. From Seb as a nervous youth to a relative 'Mr Cool' now, I can still tell when the big occasion is getting to him. By God, it gets to me. In fact, it gets to me more as I experience it, not less.

Traumas: There are terrible moments when things go wrong, but others make up for them. That first [mile] world record in Oslo (3:48.95); the Olympics. Well, I could live through them all again.

Gaining coaching expertise: You look inwards firstly, at your own family. Physically, we've always been late developers. I knew Seb wouldn't always be frail and relatively weak, and when he was strong enough we'd do some proper weight training. Plus, though he was smaller than contemporaries, he usually managed to handle himself well at cross-country and road races as a colt and boy. I knew he'd only get better as he grew in height and natural strength. He was getting beaten by boys who were physiologically almost men in those days. Without naming names, I can think of them now, and they've gone. Gone without trace. The Steve Ovetts of this world, who are born big, are successful early, and who maintain that through the age groups, are very rare. You really do have to soldier on with a lot of kids before you discover their full potential.

But you can go over the top a little at times. I wrote to Gordon Surtees of the BMC asking for advice. I expected that magic schedule that we all wait for – the formula that will work for you. (There are no formulas for everyone. Plenty of recipes, but no formulas.) Instead I got a nice letter couched in friendly terms stating, in a nutshell, that with this level of achievement so far, why was I seeking to give the lad a bigger workload? As this wasn't what I wanted to hear, it went on the scrapshelf. Three days later I went back to it when my ruffled feathers had been smoothed and analysed it objectively. I thought, 'well, the fellow has to be right'. In the nicest way, Gordon slowed me down. It never hurts to listen to advice. Always listen and act or reject as you think fit. But if you don't listen, you may not hear.

Seeking other help: We used Frank Horwill's idea of multi-tiered training. After Frank wrote to me of this method, Seb trained at 400, 800, 1,500 and 3,000 metre pace over a fourteen day period in the essential build-up phase after the winter. Now we work at 400, 800, 1,500 and 5,000 metre pace. Frank's ideas made complete sense to me. I think we are on the right road, and nine world records tend to back me up on that. . . .

But you miss things. Wilf Paish spotted a weakness once as Seb finished a race, and suggested he needed more 300 metre reps in training. When I analysed this, I found he was quite right. Seb could always manage good 200 and 400 reps, but 300s were anything but a screaming success. We worked on them after that, because here was an obvious weakness. You must strengthen your weak areas, but don't overdo it because it can become counterproductive. Always play to your strengths. The strengths are what make an athlete go. Now 300s are a very good indicator to me of Seb's level of fitness.

Racing: It's not winning that's important so much as HOW you win. You can go on winning for a long time by carefully putting yourself into graded races, but the most important thing that happened to Seb was getting into fast races in 1975-76 and getting screwed. Many times he tore off for three laps and then got caught up in a cavalry charge over the last 300 metres. But he was *learning* all the time. Brendan Foster told him: 'Don't worry, Seb. It will come right for you in the end.' Eventually he knew he'd be able to run 'em off their feet from any position in the field. Don't you, as youngsters, get carried away with the importance of tactics. Tactics are for those who are masters of the job. Give of your best, take them all on, and find out about your strengths and weaknesses. Learn to commit yourself early on. Life doesn't end if you get beaten at times. You need to learn to lose before you can win big. Learning to commit yourself was an important part of the BMC philosophy that we picked up early on. It's HOW you win that is important.

World records: A world record is a moving target. You have to sit down and work out where it's going to be when you are ready for it. Statistics properly used here can be a big help, and it's worthwhile looking up the average age of the top people in your event. I worked out where between ages sixteen and twenty-two (for Seb) the world records would be. I was on for most of them, but the 1,500 metres has not improved to around 3:30.0 as I thought it would by now. Certainly anyone who can finish a mile race in 3:47.33 the way Seb did in Brussels in 1981 can run 3:30 for 1,500. We over-achieved on the 800 record, taking it below 1:42.00, on the other hand. If you achieve your yearly targets, be satisfied; don't get greedy and go for more. You can overdo the workload with youngsters for nothing more than personal ego. I ease Seb off even now, if I see he is really going well. I'll tell him to stop, for instance, if I've seen enough after four reps, instead of letting him finish the full six. You are always nursing an athlete through, not trying to expend him.

Injuries/illnesses: Seb went through the entire year with bad sciatic pains in 1980, and we had to prepare for Moscow through it all. In 1981, things went really well, and we couldn't have asked for a better trouble-free season. Results proved it. In 1982 – injury again. It happens. You have to adopt the training that will allow you to recover without breaking down again, and this will restrict you at times.

Seb took the bronze medal in the 1975 European Junior 1,500 in Athens on 28½ miles per week average, whilst the winner was on 70 miles per week. In Prague (1978) he was recovering from a very bad foot injury which depressed the mileage to 35 miles per week. How he got back so fast is still a mystery – that was a shocker of an injury. In Athens this year he almost pulled it off on very restricted training again due to injury. We were really playing poker with a very poor hand. He had no background work to fall back on and it caught up with him with just 80 metres to go in the final. I never can see that race in the same terms as Moscow (800), because in Athens he did everything right, whereas in Moscow he ran a terrible tactical race.

Speed/strength training: We will modify his sessions this winter because nothing should be static in training and you want to progress as much as possible until you plateau out. You have to match the strength and experience against the fact that physically your athlete may be slowing up. You cannot escape from speed, and that comes from strength. And you cannot run fast if you are weak. I maintain that a top class middle-distance runner must have a good 400-metre time. Frank Horwill has written many times that leg speed equals strength. The way to assess anaerobic quality is by measuring leg strength (Lewis Nonogram Test).

The gym work at Loughborough was ideal for Seb to increase his leg power and overall strength. I talked it over with George Gandy and he and Seb embarked on a rigorous circuit schedule. He also developed good weight lifting technique to protect him from damage/injuries. Now he does squats with 180lb on his back in sets of six, which is not bad considering he only weighs around 130lb. But he has run a 400-metre relay in a short 45 (45.5), which indicates leg speed gained from strength. Ally that speed to specific speed/endurance work, and you come up with a sub 1:42 for 800 metres.

The breakthrough in Seb's speed came about with really well applied gym work. His power/weight ratio is very good and he also possesses good speed and flexibility. He maintains cadence at speed through strength and flexibility. So we used George Gandy's knowledge of biomechanics and gym circuits and John Humphreys' Physiological Testing Centre at Leeds extensively. We found that sticking to the same work physiologist makes the findings comparable. Other doctors may come up with differing results from the same tests, through using different apparatus and routines. We constantly monitor his VO_2 uptake, haemoglobin etc.

On the Coe family: It always pays to have an intelligent mother. And I counted the females in the room before I made that sexist remark! Angela (Coe) spots things in her children that others may miss, and she can always tell when Sebastian may be slightly unwell or not his usual self. So I always consult her. 'Well how does he look to you today?' We are a close family, we respect talent, and we like achievers. Seb found out that when he was good at something, it gave him a spin-off into other areas through the genuine pride he had in himself. And sports psychologists have findings which support this in fact.

I prefer to be known as Seb's coach rather than his father. Parenthood is fairly commonplace. Being lucky and privileged enough to coach a world class athlete is pretty rare. I'm probably more proud of being his coach than I am in being his father.

Moscow, 1980: This was crunch time. There was no more restraint. The records all counted for nothing here; winning was all-important. The 800-metre silver, for me, was a failure. I've always supported Ian Stewart's view that 'First is first, and second is nowhere'. This outlook doesn't suit everybody, but it seems logical to me for people who have a genuine expectation of winning. This is a bit harsh, bit cruel, bit arrogant, but it's what I think such an athlete needs.

I noted from his clumsiness just beforehand that something was getting to him, that he wasn't totally relaxed about his race preparation. He was not locked in, concentrating totally on the job in hand. But he was so far better than any of the other 800 metre finalists that I couldn't see him losing unless he was really badly off form. And I couldn't see him being that bad. So I was faced with the choice of saying something to him just before the race, or staying quiet, although I knew he was not quite right. That's a hell of a position for a coach, minutes before the big race. Perhaps if I'd said something he might have snapped out of the trance he was in, and run with more awareness than he did. But then again, I might have made him worse. In the event, I said nothing, and to this day I'll never know if I did the right thing or not. Coaching is a case of trying to maximize the rights, and minimize the wrongs, and hoping to get it right most of the time. That's all you can ever hope to do.

Watching the heats and semis of the 1,500 metres, on the other hand, I knew there was no way he could lose the final. And a journalist who was close to us (David Miller) saw it too, *because* he was close. He was the only reporter to predict that Seb would win. Seb's attitude to the 1,500 metres was so different, because the first trauma was over and out of his system. He knew he couldn't run as badly again. This one was watsit or bust. He wouldn't get another chance for four years. And you'd better do at least half of what you set out to do. He went there to pull both titles, and I think he should have done.

Televised spectaculars: We like them on the whole because we are largely removed from problems with team officials, and people who always mean well but just end up getting in the flaming way. But we haven't got the formula right over here [in Britain]. Somehow the atmosphere is not quite what you would expect, even with thirty great athletes at the meeting. I remember the White City meetings as having more atmosphere than Crystal Palace. It's the old story of the prophet not being accepted in his own land. At meetings abroad (Oslo, Zurich, Stockholm) we are always treated much better and allowed the freedom of the stadium. At Crystal Palace, it's 'No! You can't go here, and you can't go there!'

Conclusion: The great conditioner is 5,000 metre training. I find it essential for the late winter/early spring phase. If you can cope with the demands of 5,000 metre pace work, you will be able to cope with all racing schedules – heats, semis, finals, all close together. You don't have to hammer big mileages necessarily, but tailor a 5,000 schedule to your level of development, and you won't go far wrong.

Letter from Peter Coe to *Athletics Weekly*:

There is a myth being spread that Sebastian has a secret training method. In fact, according to Peter Hildreth in the *Sunday Telegraph* it is so good that it saves him from using drugs to beat the world's best and I have a duty to disclose this secret to the coaching world in order to save our youth from the dreaded pills (why not have a simple moral objection?). An alternative 'secret' was disclosed in a strip in the *Sunday Times* which suggests that their illustrated exploits of Seb's rope-climbing, box-bounding, striding and leaping are the reason for his success. Why do I feel so concerned over articles about which it could be said that they only purport to show how great is my athlete? Because they can easily fool youth and enthusiastic athletes and, even worse, whether the writers realize it or not, they cast a slur on professional coaches and the BAAB coaching system. I have also seen this rubbish published in American running magazines headed 'Seb's Secret Training'. I think it is worth noting here that I am the *only* coach Sebastian has ever had from the day he first started running. No one else has had any say of any kind in his training, racing programme or in the compilation of a planned career on the country, road or track. If anyone knew of a secret it would be me, and I would have thought that any searcher for the 'great truth' would have asked me and not other people.

Before Seb even saw Loughborough University, I met George Gandy and got his agreement to supervise Seb's circuit and weight training, which George has done carefully and meticulously. That's long-term planning. Seb was never an athlete away from home, lost and looking for advice – that's not my style. A coach should build a back-up team: we have our own favourite and proven physiotherapists at our three working bases, Sheffield, Leicester and London. Physiological advice is available in Leeds and Loughborough. But only *one* coach. No athlete will succeed when listening to too many people. Only one can call the shots.

Now about motivation. If you are not self-motivated you are wasting your time, and everyone else's. No coach can be giving you his best attention if he has to wonder if you will turn up or carry out his instructions when you are on your own. Instead of working on your improvement, he's wasting his emotional and nervous energy. Emotional? Yes, because he must believe passionately in what he's doing. Not for me the aloof and distant pose. I can't run the races, but by God I'm involved in winning. This search for 'secrets' and 'gimmicks' obscures the fact that there is not any short cut to the top. Not one. Symptomatic of this search for magic was the insulting idea that if we wanted medals in the Olympics and other major Championships we should send our athletes abroad to foreign coaches. East Germany was suggested for example. How on earth did Wells, Thompson, Ovett, Coe, Oakes and our girls ever manage their medal achievements? Are we so conditioned to failure that secretly we need to find excuses for success? Are we really so timid? At world level, athletics is currently our most successful sport, above all others.

I can give any athlete the recipe for success, but it is not the magic formula. It's only the list of ingredients. They are, in order of importance: Talent (there is no substitute for this), Motivation, Dedication and Loyalty. Loyalty to a coach is very important. Why don't I mention beating a path to the door at Loughborough? Because there isn't anything new there in the gymnasium or weight room. When I showed the *Sunday Times* strip to Seb he laughed and said, 'I've been doing it for years, along with forty to eighty others, some of whom do the exercises better than I do.' So it can't be there. Why don't I write down my secret training, sell it, and retire for life, rich, anywhere in the world. For one very good reason and one only . . . it does not exist!

Seb is trained in an orthodox fashion using known methods. A coach, I believe it was Harry Wilson, once said that coaches get a reputation for knowing a lot about athletes, when in reality they know a lot about some athletes. And that is a very large part of coaching: knowing the athlete intimately. Choose a coach carefully, and unless you are totally certain your coach is not the one for you, stick with him. Chopping and changing tells more about you than the coach. His success depends so much on continuity. My success with Seb is only possible through his loyalty to me, wherein I can experiment slowly (only varying one factor at a time) and check my results. I use a basic five-tier training system, which I discussed with Frank Horwill as long ago as 1971:

The way I use 300 metre sessions was influenced by Wilf Paish.

My little knowledge of physiology is enhanced by Dr John Humphreys and others. These people's work is freely available.

When I attended coaching conferences, so did many others, we all drew from the same pool.

I build Seb's programme year by year with the bricks of my training – Frank Dick would call this periodizing – using micro and macro cycles.

The energy systems I seek to develop and use are those explained in the publications of work-physiologists. The duration and intensity of the stimuli is known to many others.

What is special is only that Seb's training is tailored specifically to him and his requirements by a coach who is in a unique position of being able to have detailed knowledge of his charge. My point is that there are not any magic formulae. A logical, intelligent application of widely-known facts, damned hard work by an athlete and coach alike, no neglected details, meticulous care, dedication . . . these are the requirements. If I bring anything new to coaching, it is what I said in a seminar in America eighteen months ago: think like a good modern industrial manager, identify your short-term and long-term objectives, marshal your resources and co-ordinate your help. Above all think first, and then act with conviction. In the UK all that we require are better facilities and nationally organized sports medicine as a back-up for our coaches.

Why not for once opt for the simple explanation? Endowed by nature with the right equipment, loyal to one coach (this has given me time to succeed), dedicated to hard training and being totally disciplined, Seb has become, simply, very good at his job. In other words, Sebastian Coe *has made himself* better than the rest. That is the lesson for all to see.

Five

Recovering against the Clock

It was unsurprising that the New Year's Eve party given by Seb should include several people from the medical and orthopaedic field who were helping him overcome his most depressing twenty months in fifteen predominantly successful years of running. He readily admitted that the path back to the Olympic Games in Los Angeles would be infinitely harder than the recovery he made after defeat in the 800 metres in Moscow to win the 1,500 metres five days later. He could not be *sure* yet that he would run in Los Angeles. It had taken a psychological adjustment to come to terms with the fact that anything he could still achieve would be a bonus after the set-backs of the last two summers. By now, however, he could look upon his situation in a reasonable mood. 'You could say that Moscow had previously been my toughest mental hurdle, but this is something much deeper,' he said, while his friends tried to give the occasion a mood of levity. 'Some of the other competitors in the Olympics will be four to six years younger than I am, and may have been fitter, harder and faster than I will have been during the months beforehand. But any pressure there is must be only from me, not from the public. Pressure is only what you allow to get through to you. I remember first going into the empty Lenin Stadium, a track which I like, but it seemed somehow ominous, like a boxing ring, an appointment closing in on me. When I recently went to the Los Angeles Coliseum, during a visit to America with my father, I simply felt free, and hopeful.'

Not long ago a friend, conscious of Seb's depression, had jolted him into reassessment by reminding him that he was no sixth form drop-out, but a current world record holder. What was important was that by now he had mentally reached a point where he was prepared to make a monumental effort once more, while recognizing that he might fall short of success. He still winced, however, at the continuing cynicism in the occasional newspaper column, referring in New Year reflections upon 1983 and 1984 to his '*mystery*' illness.

His biopsy and blood tests had revealed that he was suffering from a cat-borne disease, *acquired toxoplasmosis*. He had it in the lymphatic form, said to be mild, which has symptoms similar to glandular fever: swollen glands, muscle pains, a temperature, and a general feeling of being unwell. Recovery can be slow, and occasionally the disease becomes chronic, sometimes acute in people whose resistance has been lowered. All animals can be infected by *toxoplasmosis* – the Coe family dog was tested and found to be negative. But it is only in the cat's gut that the parasitic protozoa, *toxoplasma condii*, reproduces. The oocytes which form there are passed into the cat's faeces, which can then contaminate badly stored food, or unwashed hands. At least it was clear that a specific, known disease had caused the relapse in form, probably for two summers. The condition was *not* the product of too much running or training.

However, what had been discovered in addition to this disease, was that Seb had developed a serious displacement of the lower back. This condition was being treated twice a week by Cynthia Tucker, a prominent osteopath, whose clients included the Wimbledon champion John McEnroe. She was present at the party, and confirmed in conversation that Seb's muscular counter-stresses had been radically altering his proper posture. 'For most of last summer I could never produce any change of pace in the last lap, it hurt too much,' Seb told me. 'There were times when it was painful to walk. It seemed the trouble was in my stomach, and I had had a scan two weeks before I was beaten in Paris. Then I discovered it came from my back, the same problem that was nagging in 1980, and happily I'm now moving better than at any time since 1981. I suppose its the accumulation of fourteen years of severe training. People were starting to talk last July about *mental* weakness, but all the time I just knew that the weakness was that I was nowhere near the physical condition

I had once been in. Considering that I ran under 1:44 last summer in spite of the shape I was in, I'm reasonably optimistic for *this* year. I saw nothing last year to frighten me. My motivation is still to win a gold at 800 metres, though I would be happy with *any* medal at either distance. To most people, I'm someone who has failed in major championships, but I don't feel that my World Cup and two Europa Cup victories make me too bad a runner. I'll have to play it by ear now, phase by phase, and see whether I'm ready for the trials in June. I feel that ought to be the deciding race.' Seb had been pre-selected for the 800 metres, but he did not know yet whether he would be in shape to challenge for the one spare place in the 1,500 metres, for which Ovett and Cram had been pre-selected.

Steve Mitchell, a gregarious school teacher from north-east London, with whom Seb had shared a house in Loughborough for some time, knows the moods and motivations of his contemporary as well or better than most. 'In the period from August to Christmas when he was not running, I think he *thought* that he could get back, and his close friends mostly considered that the problem would be psychological as much as physical,' Steve told me when looking back on that difficult time. 'Seb was quite relaxed when we went on holiday to Italy, as much as anything he wanted to get away from the coverage of the World Championships. Like most athletes, if he's injured he's not a good spectator. There's no doubt that he was hurt by the way some people had dismissed him, and he's still got some of the articles in his bedroom, though he never talked much about it. He took his medication treatment very seriously, and gave great care to following the routines, even though some of the time he was feeling pretty sick. Looking back to last summer when things were not going too well, the way he kept his determination was extraordinary. He would not contemplate that illness could be a cause. When he lost to Zdravkovic, and then to Scott, there was still no thought of illness, that I could detect. It was only when he lost at Gateshead that he would at last accept the possibility that he was unwell. During the times when it was going badly, he would sit in the kitchen with Peter, sometimes till two in the morning, discussing the situation, but they still hadn't considered the medical side [hospital reports after the Athens illness had suggested that all was clear]. There were occasionally heated exchanges, but Seb would always stand up for himself. Some people have got the idea that he's dominated by his father, but that's simply not true.

'Early in 1984 his training was going quite well, the same sort of distance work as usual for the time of year. He didn't talk about his feelings very much, he put the summer at the back of his mind. Long term things with him are kept very much *long* term. For the past few winters, it's mostly been distance running and hill work, so his approach to 1984 was much the same, except that he started later and had none of the indoor track races. His main concern through March and April, I think, was whether Chelsea were going to get promotion. His interest in that was something which helped take his mind off other things. Where he did think about his prospects for the summer, I had the impression that he recognized a lot of athletes train more than they have to, only because everyone *else* does, and that therefore he might not have lost too much. For instance, when Cram won the World Championships, he wasn't fit until just before. Yet there was a slight anxiety apparent in Seb. When he went to Sutton Coldfield for a road relay in April, it was a bit windy and difficult, something that wouldn't normally have bothered him, but he was obviously rather tense for an event that was fairly ordinary, where his performance wouldn't tell him very much. Yet I knew before he went away to Chicago before the Games, that he was in as good a shape as he'd ever been.'

Much of the encouragement during the period of rehabilitation had come from John Hovell, a veteran coach at Haringey. His at times almost disciplinarian attitude had prevented any slackening that there might have been in Seb's will. His goading catch-phrase was 'don't think about the past, think about the future'.

During some of his training between the end of 1983 and the following spring, Seb was accompanied by Hugh Hastings, a young photographer. They had met through the Chelsea football club, for whom Hastings took pictures. Hastings observed some of the progress of the rehabilitation of a great athlete. 'When he first started in Richmond Park, he didn't know if he could make it,' recalls Hugh. 'It wasn't until he became involved on the physiology-testing treadmill at Loughborough in February and March that it was really confirmed that he would be OK. Prior to that it was a case of seeing how it went day by day. It was a battle with himself. He never showed any of the resentment he must have had towards those who had written him off. He never really discussed, that I heard, his chances if and when he got back into competition. He was just level-headed, but obviously so bloody determined to do well. I think, looking back, he knew that he could do it, and certainly there was never a time when I doubted it, from anything of the attitude he revealed to me. Nor, for that matter, from Peter who came training with him at least once a week. By degrees, I don't think his friends had any doubt either. He seldom mentioned in any discussions those whom he might be running against, except Aouita now and again. From February onwards, my opinion was increasingly that if he could get the preparation right, no one could stop him. When I met him at Gatwick on one occasion, after he had been training in the south of Spain for a week, it had obviously been going quite well, and he jokingly said, "it looks like I'll have to go on for another year then". He and Peter are two of the most determined men I have ever met.'

As Seb began to get back into the swing of things, and cause for some optimism appeared, Peter felt able to talk more freely about the strains which *he* had been under during the previous summer. 'None of the innuendoes which were going around reached me at the time. All I was aware of was that, even allowing for normal variation, there were things that Seb couldn't manage in training that he normally can do. But the severity of the disease was masked by his own determination to keep pressing on. Because there was no initial awareness of his illness, the more training he did the worse his physical condition was likely to become. The normal progress in training is that you increase the levels once the athlete can comfortably repeat the phase you are in, within only a short time, a day or two. Whether it is stamina or speed you are going for, the best sign is that the level is repeatable. But last year there was consistently no sign of this, and as coach it was therefore very confusing. Seb would run a 400 one day, and then be unable to manage a 300 at the same level a day or so later. There were two ways of looking at this situation: what could be got out of him with much less training, and how much might his own remarkable capacity to produce speed on little preparation still rescue something – as he had done in Athens the year before? I knew that no one else in his condition then could ever hope to get through even the heats.'

The obvious question therefore, had to be why the coach, knowing something was wrong, allowed the athlete to continue? It was the answer to that which demonstrated not the alleged *rift* between father and son, but the *bond*. 'It is a fundamental premise of coaching that you can only work by consent, by the athlete's agreement to do what you ask,' said Peter. 'You have to have that. But the ultimate decision to go for something has to be the athlete's. Seb was *determined* to run in the World Championships. Therefore I was obliged to do whatever I could to make that possible, and to minimize his problems. He will have my loyalty as long as he wants it. Even when he ran 1:43.8 in Oslo, I wasn't happy, yet I cannot pretend to greater knowledge than I had at the time. Fortunately, the faith between us is such that it is now possible for us to joke about last summer, the realization that it was doomed to failure. The mistake I made last year, towards the end, was to be too protective when Seb was under pressure from the media as the defeats started to come. I could see the pressure becoming another nail in the coffin.'

Eight months is a long time for an athlete of Seb's calibre to go without any kind of race. It was on 31 March, competing for his new club Haringey in a road relay at Cranford in Middlesex, that he returned to the flavour of running against opposition. In biting cold he ran his three-and-three-quarter-mile leg in 16 minutes 16 seconds – almost four-minute-mile pace, and the fastest leg recorded by any of the 350 athletes taking part. He had decided over two weeks previously to take part, but no announcement had been made because he wanted to keep public attention to a minimum. 'I haven't been as happy for a long time,' he said afterwards. 'If I continue to make the same progress, then I can consider getting back into track competition in reasonable time. Obviously I'm still several weeks behind most other people aiming for the Olympics, but I've been improving steadily and it was time to test the water. It was exhilarating being able to go past people once again, and the most encouraging thing is that I seem to have suffered no physical reaction.'

A week after Cranford, Seb was running in the Southern Counties road relay championships at Wimbledon, and a fortnight after that in the National AAA Championships at Sutton Coldfield. Running the fourth of twelve stages of 3.1 miles he lifted Haringey from eleventh to fifth, before they eventually fell back to finish ninth behind Tipton Harriers. He was only a second slower than the fastest man of the day, Mark O'Reilly of Highgate, on the shorter of two distances which competitors had to cover. Three weeks after that, gingerly returning to the track, Seb ran the second leg for Haringey in a 4 x 400 metres relay in the GRE League at Wolverhampton. His split of 46.74 was respectable enough, and now he could contemplate a race proper: the Middlesex Championships at Enfield a week later, when he would test his nerve over 800 metres. The outer perimeters of Middlesex were not accustomed to this sort of spectacle: the man trying to piece together his jinxed career produced the then fastest time in the world for the year with 1:45.2, winning by some 30 metres after leading at the bell in 52. Yet he could tell that there was still a long way to go: for someone not normally extended by a race at even such a pace as this, he found he was actually *sweating*. We had seen him with barely a bead of perspiration when he broke the world mile record for the third time in his last great run almost three years previously. 'My fitness is still only about seventy per cent,' he said cautiously.

To test the endurance factor, he now moved up, a fortnight further on, to 1,500 metres in the Southern Counties Championships at Crystal Palace on 1 and 2 June. To run in a heat would be good for his training, and he needed to give the selectors good warning if he considered himself a serious candidate for both events in Los Angeles. The team was due to be finalized on 25 or 26 June, immediately following the AAA Championships and, as everyone knew, there was only one spare place for the 1,500 metres alongside Ovett and Cram. There was no 1,500 metres included in the Olympic trials at Crystal Palace and Gateshead in the week following that race in the Southern Counties meeting – which the Olympic champion won, with a 53 last lap, in 3:43.11, ahead of Eamonn Martin, the UK 5,000 metres champion. Privately, Seb did not think he had run particularly well, and to his friends it was apparent, down on the track-side after the race, that he was ill at ease. But if he had the makings of problems, so too did Ovett, who also wanted to double up in LA, but was now ruled out of the following Wednesday's Olympic 800 trial because of bronchitis.

Opposition for the spare 1,500 metres place was brewing for Seb from Elliott who, having won himself an 800 selection in the Olympic trials on 8 June, now ambitiously planned to expand his range to the unfamiliar four laps and to confront Seb in the AAA 1,500, after first testing his four-lap ability in the Emsley Carr Mile, which was included in the second day of Olympic trials at Gateshead. Elliott's reputation was not to be treated lightly. In 1983 he had been European indoor silver medallist, was an outstanding fourth in the World Championships at 800 metres, and had raced the distance no fewer than thirty times in the year with a remarkable seventeen performances proving better than the Olympic standard time of 1:47. Yet, continually in the shadow of publicity and acclaim for the British 'big three', he was apt to be regarded as on the proverbial chopping block. Now twenty-one, he was impatient to shake a few feathers; and one way to do this was to oust Coe from the Olympic 1,500 metres. His coach, Wilf Paish, was convinced he had the ability to do so, and was encouraging his athlete to go after the big names, looking for a showdown.

Elliott, a steel worker from Rotherham, enjoys his reputation as a conventional Yorkshireman: bluff and direct, though mostly quietly spoken. He likes to be thought of as the man who does a full working shift, and fits his athletics around that in the old fashioned way. There is much to be said for his transparently sincere attitude, though whether he could do with more refinement in the judgement of his training and racing, both by himself and by Paish, was something only time would tell. Such judgement has nothing to do with where you were born, but how shrewdly you are able to assess your own potential. Elliott and Paish obviously considered they were on a crest and, like a surfer, wanted to keep the board riding as long as possible. I think that some of Elliott's home-spun strengths and weaknesses are apparent – for example, his dismissal of 'so-called experts' – in a sympathetic interview with Nigel Whitefield, published in *Athletics Weekly* early in 1984, from which some extracts are reproduced here:

I couldn't go to college to do a Mickey Mouse course and sit on my backside all day waiting for the next training session. It would drive me mad. I'm not interested in that sort of lifestyle. I had a week of sitting around the house all day when I broke my arm recently in the 'Superstars' competition and that was more than enough. I feel much happier at work because although it gets pretty hard as a joiner rolling around in muck all the time it does hammer home your priorities, which is a good thing. Athletics is very important to me but it's not everything; it could be all finished tomorrow if you get an unlucky break. There's no time to get bored when you're doing a 7.30am–4pm shift and trying to fit in two or three training sessions as well, but I don't want to sound like a martyr – I do enjoy it in a strange kind of way. I've got to be very grateful to my employers who are extremely helpful to me with time off and so forth.

I'm not a high mileage runner, I never have been. I don't think you have to blast 120 miles per week to run well on the track – it all depends upon the individual. I had a great season last year yet my racing was done off a very low but high quality winter mileage. The key really is to run a sensible winter and it doesn't have to include a mass of cross country racing like the *so-called experts* claim [author's italics]. I've hardly run any since I won the Youths' 'National' in 1980. I hate running it, I always have done and I always will. I'm not about to change my ways, especially now that it's obviously unnecessary. Besides, if I did go back, all the specialist country men would be falling over themselves to take my scalp, which is meaningless. Why bother? I'd much rather go out to New Zealand this winter and race there again. It was my trip out there last year which set me up for such a tremendous track season. I'm hoping to work something out again; maybe I'll be able to stay out there for a little longer than a month this time, which should leave me in great shape for Los Angeles. I've also got a £1,000 Peugeot-Talbot grant which should make things a little easier. . . .

The main thing to bear in mind about racing is that there's no point avoiding anybody; you've got to go out there and give it a bash – sure you'll have it shoved up you a few times but in the long run you'll benefit from it because that's the only way to improve. I had to race a lot last year because the British Board wanted to see what I was made of. Now they've had their way I can afford to pick and choose in the future, which is going to be quite a luxury. . . .

I thought Coe was invincible and kept holding back waiting for his inevitable kick [at Loughborough in 1983], and sure enough it came. The only reason I couldn't respond was because I didn't have enough self-belief. You've really got to believe in your ability if you're going to be able to compete on level terms with somebody like that. I was in a similar situation at Cosford when he ran 1:44.9 for a new world record. I had a good run as well but I just couldn't muster up the courage to go with him – I wish I had now.

At Gateshead it was a different story; once we'd seen signs of him faltering we were queueing up to have a run at him. It's a bit unfair, but then you can't expect any favours once the race starts. It did feel quite strange to beat the unbeatable although some of the pleasure was taken away by the fact that I ended up losing myself – again to Steve Cram. It just confirmed my suspicions that there was something wrong with Seb and so it proved. I'm not one of those fools who think he's finished. I'm sure he'll be back with a vengeance, as we might discover to our cost. . . .

It was great [the World Championships] I had nothing to lose, so I just went out there and made all the others suffer like hell . . . at least they knew they'd been in a fight, which is some consolation. Actually I didn't expect much at all; I just wanted to make the final and once I'd done that I felt like I'd achieved my goal. At the end though I was disappointed to miss out on the medal; I thought I'd got the bronze coming off the bend but it just slipped out of my grasp. It's all good experience though. I did make a conscious effort to blast through to the bell at a decent pace and I don't regret it at all. I can't run any other way. I've got to get out in the front, otherwise I don't feel comfortable.

It does make you a bit of a target, as that race shows, but I've got no alternative. I've tried to sit and kick but it just doesn't work trying to mix it with the faster guys over the last 200 metres. Besides I hate those races where we jog round the first lap then go berserk down the back straight. You've got to play to your advantages, and my strengths don't include an 11-second last 100 metres. . . .

I'm sure I'll eventually move up to 1,500 metres or the mile and I'm quite looking forward to it because I think I could do reasonably well over the longer distance. That's quite a long way off though. I've still got a lot more to do over 800 metres, and I don't want to finish with that until I've done justice to myself and registered a time with which I can feel really satisfied. Obviously I can't expect my personal best to keep coming down the way it has – it's going to get much harder to make progress from now on. Ideally I'd like to string a couple of 51 second laps together and end up with something in the region of 1:42 – it's not impossible by any means. You've got to think in those terms and be positive, otherwise you'll end up going sideways rather than forward.

I owe a great debt to Bill McRobb who coached me until 1980 and really brought me forward before sensibly and unselfishly passing me on, when he'd done all he could for me, and of course to Wilf Paish, my present coach, who has helped me a great deal. . . . Athletics is a very unpredictable thing and the chances are things won't work out the way I hope – they quite often don't and I've come to accept that. One of the most valuable lessons I've learnt in my short career to date is that you can't take anything for granted, so when I say my season is geared to the Los Angeles Games it is with no small degree of uncertainty.

Against a modest field, and with a time which improved his previous best by almost three seconds, Elliott won the Emsley Carr Mile in 3:55.71; and significantly he was three seconds faster at the 1,500 metres mark than Seb had been a week before, also producing a sharp last lap of 55.

Before the AAA Championships, Cram and Coe were due to appear in the annual match between the AAA and Loughborough. Cram was talking uncertainly about the possibility of his doubling up in LA; he would run 1,000 metres at Loughborough, and Coe, who was organizing the Sanatagon-sponsored meeting, an 800. But Seb tore some thigh fibres doing a 1,000 repetition in training, and had to withdraw in order to be sure of being fit for the AAA Championships; Ovett deputized for him. Cram duly won the 1,000 metres at Loughborough, confirmed he would run 800 in the AAA Championships, but decided he would abandon any idea of chasing two events in LA, whatever his performance. Ovett won the 800 at Loughborough but it was evident, in spite of a fast second lap, that he was still worryingly impeded by respiratory and muscular problems. To convince the British that they would need to be at a peak a month or so later, if they needed any convincing, some impressive results were being recorded overseas, notably by Donata Sabia, a twenty-year-old Italian, who ran the fastest 800 of the year with 1:43.88 in Florence to beat Druppers and Juantorena; and, also in Florence, an exceptional 13:04.78 for 5,000 by Aouita. Then there was an 800 in the US Olympic trials in Los Angeles in which four men ran under 1:44. Earl Jones set a US record of 1:43.74, shared with Johnny Gray in second place, while James Robinson found himself out of the Olympics with 1:43.92 behind John Marshall. In the same meeting, Carl Lewis warmed up the bookmakers' odds on his projected four gold medals, with a long jump of 28 feet 7 inches and a 200 metres in 19.84.

If Ovett was happy to leave it to the selectors whether or not to nominate him for the 800 metres, following his victory at Loughborough (and another a few days later in Belfast), preferring to concentrate on training rather than getting involved with Cram, Juantorena and Cook in the AAA 800, there was no way Coe could avoid his public examination against Elliott. With some ambiguity – the responsibility for which could never be firmly pinned on any door – the Coe-Elliott race had been widely billed as an Olympic trial, though that had never been the intention of the British Board. Obviously such a prospect would help fill seats at Crystal Palace for the AAA. Yet, reading between the many lines – which became inextricably crossed in the controversy about to develop – it can be said with reasonable certainty that the Olympic champion had been told he had to do no more than show himself to be fit. That would seem a correct concession. No one could deny that Coe had unavoidably begun his preparations late, was engaged in a racing schedule which would reach its peak only in time for the Olympics, and that it made no sense to be fighting out a domestic event five weeks before the Olympics. But it made sense enough to Elliott that a decision should be taken according to who was the first man home. Seb could do nothing but concur publicly with such a sentiment, and certainly he intended and expectated to be able to beat Elliott at this moment, whatever sort of race it was. Commenting on the prospects beforehand, Cram had said: 'If everything is right, I feel that can only be one winner – Coe. But you have to give Elliott the credit for having a go.' The pressure was certainly all on Coe, who had been having daily physiotherapy on his thigh injury, and said he had decided to run only because he wished to defend his Olympic title: 'and the way to do that is to prove to everyone that I am ready for the task'.

It proved to be an unmemorable, slow and rough race, with runners regularly bargeing into each other among a field of twelve. In the first lap Coe was pushed by a young Frenchman, Laventure, and on the second lap, entering the home straight, he nearly went down, lungeing sideways after seemingly being buffeted from behind by Williamson. Elliott was spiked in both legs, and ran a tactically unintelligent race in a vulnerable position behind the leaders. Eamonn Martin led at 400 in 58.5 and Laventure at 800 in a fraction under two minutes. Down the last back straight, Elliott went ahead followed by Coe and Williamson; coming off the final bend Coe made his move, coming through on the inside to lead by a couple of strides and he seemed to have the race won. He did not have enough in hand.

Elliott is nothing if not brave. He clawed his way back over the last few metres, at the end of a final lap in 55, to become the first man ever to beat Coe at both 800 metres and 1,500 metres. It was the result, not the manner of the performance, which made many of the newspapers next morning predict that the steel worker had hammered the university economist out of an Olympic place. It was, in fact, only Elliott's fourth race at the distance, but he gave his victory as much inflation as he could by saying that he definitely wished to double up, and he understood the selectors decision would be based on the day's result. Yet 3:39.66, only hundredths ahead of Coe, was hardly a conclusive time, whatever excitement it might have produced for a 12,000 crowd. Reactions and comments varied substantially. Pat Butcher in *The Times* thought that Elliott's victory was probably going to prevent Coe from defending his Olympic title, and he read as much into Coe's immediate congratulation of the winner, though Butcher added that Elliott's reaction was to 'wait and see'. Neil Wilson in the *Daily Mail* wrote that Elliott's victory did nothing to prove that he was good enough for an Olympic double attempt, only that Coe was not. Defeat, said Wilson, should make Coe concentrate exclusively on the 800 metres, for which he was already selected, and that 'only the greatest Olympians have successfully attempted the 800 and 1,500 at the same Games and none has succeeded since Peter Snell in 1964'. Coe's only comment had been a diplomatic: 'there's nothing for me to say, it's Peter's day.' Ken Mays in the *Daily Telegraph* reported Elliott as saying: 'I won't make any fuss or protests if they decide to leave me out. That will be their choice, but I feel I have proved something . . . that I have finished my apprenticeship.' In the *Daily Express*, David Emery considered that 'the race proved nothing, except that they never come back'.

The only substantially dissenting voice in the general mood came from John Rodda in *The Guardian*, who said that he hoped the horizons of the eight selectors would go far beyond the previous day's combat. There was, he argued, an enormous catalogue of evidence from earlier to be considered:

In the end, the verdict should unquestionably go down in favour of the world record breaker and Olympic champion, who showed the crowd of 12,000, together with the selectors, that after injury and illness he is coming back as one of the world's greatest middle-distance runners. The alternative is to take yesterday's evidence on its own, in which Elliott came through . . . in the modest time of 3:39.66. It is evidence that warps the truth. It is a view that is blinkered. Elliott, supremely fit, won . . . against a man who should clearly find a lot more pace and poise through the training of the next three or four weeks. Elliott has been in this position before and suffered the bad end of the verdict. He is a courageous front runner, who will need all his mind and energy for the 800 in LA. He is already selected for that, and at the end of it, I suspect he will be battered down as so often before. The selectors should turn to class and quality and take no count of the popular rebuff such a wise decision will encounter.

It was a defending QC's adroit and accurate summing up.

We cannot know whether the selectors read *The Guardian*, but they took the same point of view, duly encountering the popular wrath which Rodda had predicted. 'Snub for man who beat Coe' roared the front page of the *Daily Mail*, claiming that Elliott accused the selectors of bias on the grounds that he came from Sheffield and that it might have been different 'if I'd been born south of Watford' – an argument which conveniently overlooked the fact that Seb had lived almost all his entire running life in Sheffield. 'It's the name Seb Coe, isn't it? He is a favourite and a hero. Me, I'm a working class lad with an accent that marks me down as coming from a long way north of Watford. Perhaps if I didn't work here [at Tinsley Steel Works] and I had hundreds of university degrees, it might have made the difference.' How much encouragement, one wondered, was Elliott given to become embroiled in such a class-conscious nuance? The same vein appeared on the *Mail's* back page, and also in the *Daily Express*, in which Elliott's coach, Paish, complained: 'It stinks. Peter's been denied the chance to prove himself the best middle-distance runner in the world.' David Emery, the *Express* columnist, rightfully drew attention to the race now being seen as a charade, with the suspicion that the counterfeit confrontation was encouraged for the sake of sponsors and TV. 'Verdict goes to Coe despite the late evidence against him' was the headline in *The Times* over Butcher's story, but Rodda in *The Guardian* welcomed what he regarded as the selectors' correct decision: 'The skirmish at Crystal Palace was not the correct place to bury the Olympic champion.' Saying that the selection committee should be reduced in future to a number recognizably answerable for their actions so that the athletes and everyone else could understand what was going on, Rodda predicted that Elliott would probably run four hard races at 800 in LA and finish up without a medal, which was 'not the frame of mind in which to tackle the second event. Coe can produce evidence of coming back from defeat and winning at 1,500 metres.' Correct again!

In defending the Board's position, Frank Dick, the chief coach, explained: 'The selectors looked at the past and present records of both athletes, and at the conclusion voted that Coe was the athlete to go.' Ovett, for all his manifest problems, was named with Coe and Elliott for the 800 metres. Cram, having won the AAA 800 when coming to an abrupt halt at the finishing line with an Achilles tendon injury, scratched from the Oslo meeting, due to take place three days later, and at which Seb was due to run his favourite two laps, and Ovett the 1,500. Elliott, nursing his indignation, went to Brussels the following Sunday for a 1,500 – partly in search of a rebuff for the selectors. One would have supposed that what he needed at this stage of the season, being restricted to one event in LA, was a sprint rather than a grind – perhaps a 400 metres. The only place to prove anything now was in LA. Was Paish doing the right thing for him?

Arriving in Oslo, Seb carefully tried to steer clear of further inflaming the argument when he said that the only proper answer to any criticism would be to do his talking with his feet. He said he had only been seventy per cent fit at the start of the season, was now up to about eighty per cent, and in the next six weeks had got to get it together mentally and physically to find the other twenty per cent. He was looking for something better than the 1:44.2 which he had run a month ago in his first race of the season, because he expected the 800 in Los Angeles to be far faster, with the possibility that 1:45 might not be enough to qualify for the final.

He took a firm stride towards justifying himself on all fronts when he ran his most authoritative race for three years the following night, with a time of 1:43.84 – a time which only Jones and Gray had beaten that year, in the US trials. Coming off the final bend Coe unleashed that peerless acceleration which he had not shown for three summers, to race away from the redoubtable James Robinson, the man who had missed US selection by the thickness of his vest. In that kind of mood, Coe had seemed in the past to be unbeatable, and watching him on this occasion on television in the press room at the Wimbledon Tennis Championships, I knew that we were witnessing the renaissance of a great athlete. Afterwards he said that he was not yet fully convinced of his own suitability for the 1,500 metres in LA, and that if by 18 July, the official closing date for entries, he was not in proper shape, he would let the Board know in good time. 'I will not be a dog in the manger,' he said. On the same night, Ovett continued with his see-saw fluctuations of fitness, winning an excellently judged 1,500 in 3:34.49, ahead of such able men as Gonzalez and Flynn.

Yet we have run slightly ahead of the story. The change in Seb's mood and performance in the space of four days, between his defeat at Crystal Palace and his almost brazen victory in Oslo, followed a fundamental reappraisal of attitudes to training and the final approach to the Olympics, after lengthy and amicable discussions between him and his father. Peter was not in Oslo, and therein lay a major change between them in psychological tactics.

Six

The Ultimate Weaning

Seb has often said that anyone who tried to detect a rift between him and his father was daft. Over recent years I have been able to observe too many moments of mutual regard, and even affection, between two grown men to know that such speculation was indeed nonsense. Of course there were arguments, of course there were differences, as they tried to find the ultimate formula for the ultimate performance – which no one can ever find, but to which they at times have come close. The change in Seb as a person as well as as an athlete over the past three years has been quite distinct: repeated failure, by his own standards, accompanied by the disenchantment of sections of the media and public, produced in him an even harder streak than was already there. He had, in an expression favoured among chroniclers of the boxing ring, become mean. The two months prior to the 1984 Olympics were indeed a turning point in character and career. Seb discussed with me a couple of times before and after the Los Angeles Games what had happened during that period with Peter, and the following is an amalgam of those talks, much of which has previously appeared in the columns of *The Times*:

> Since the start of the year I'd always been effectively one stage or so behind what I would have wished, not having run from July to Christmas last year. I was low-key until March, and didn't get on the track until June. The hard works on hills was done in April rather than February. Therefore I couldn't afford to give too much time to racing, because I needed the training basis to produce the sustained performance which would be necessary over seven condensed races. I would have liked one or two more 1,500s in May and June, but at

my level of running I cannot easily use races for training because, without meaning to be egotistical, such races become a bit of a cup final for everyone else who wants to beat me, and the pressure of my own pride in what I do can then result in my having to run faster than I really intend on the day. Even in Oslo just after the defeat by Elliott, I trained on the day of the race and again the next day. But if I was going to get to the Olympics, I had to get there in one piece, and therefore I had to avoid the added stress of too much racing even when I actually needed it.

At Christmas I had thought I had almost no chance, and in March I was still doubtful. I was padding around the streets, running a few road races with Haringey, which gave me hope. The three mile leg in the national relay particularly encouraged me, because it was comparable with the sort of times which Foster and Ian Stewart used to do. I felt that even if the training wasn't that great, I would still be able to put it together in competition by August.

In April, I started repetitions on the track, on less basic work and with less emphasis on speed than usual, yet I found that at 200 metres, within a few weeks, I was going as fast or even fasther than in 1981. So it was not a bleak situation. Temperamentally, my expectations were on the up, after two years in which I had been kidding people that I had done the work when I hadn't. That sort of pretence, keeping up a front, becomes very, very tiring, the drain of the effort. In Paris when I came second in '83, and even when I ran fast in Oslo a few days later, I was trying to put on a good face when feeling awful.

One of the difficulties in sport is that positive results are magnified, yet negative things can be magnified too. So that when I came to the Southern Counties 1,500 this year, I was still thinking about '83: would I be turned over in the final 100 metres again, the area of a race which I had always previously considered to be *my* platform? I was terribly uptight for the final, after an easy heat, and ran a very nervous race. Sean Butler and Steve Mitchell both noticed I wasn't relaxed. Friends who've run and trained with you get to know your style and technique intimately. Sean, who had spent a lot of time running with me in 1980–81 and saw all my domestic races, didn't feel there was now much wrong with my training, but that I was knotted when racing.

I *had* been training reasonably well, the sessions with Peter since the AAA road relay were good, as good as I'd ever run. I didn't have quite the strength I'd had in earlier years, but I was into areas of repetition I'd never touched before. Yet in the AAA race against Elliott I ran several seconds slower than I was capable of at that stage. I got knocked around in the race, when if I had been confident I would probably have belted somebody. I saw the video afterwards, something I rarely do so soon, and I could see that my shoulders and neck were locked, my stride length was choppy, and I was heavy on my heels. Six weeks away from the Olympics, and here I was trying for both events. I had to get a grip on myself. What I was looking at in that video was the shell of a runner. It was a shock.

Afterwards Peter said that the problem now was mental: 'The physical problems of two years have compounded themselves, you've no confidence.' We spent many hours discussing it. I knew I'd got into a nose-dive, especially at 1,500, and training itself was not going to pull me out. The day after the Southern Counties, in which I'd felt washed out, I'd run some particularly fast repetitions from 1,200, through 800 down to 400. Peter recognized the contradiction that was there. He's always emphasized that I was coach-orientated and not coach-dependent. I've always been self-motivated.

I knew now that I had to present myself with a challenge which in a way was *bigger* than the Olympics. I'd just been turned over in the domestic championships in a time I was running when I was eighteen. I was nervous and frightened. So Peter and I decided that the only thing to do was for me to get off, to sort myself out on my own, and it was he who said that we should start immediately with Oslo, where he'd planned to go with me. It was one of the most important decisions we've ever made. Ultimately, it's not how coaches think or act, or what they say. It's down to you. Up to 1981, what had characterized my running was almost an arrogance, that whatever happened I would win, even though I blew it in the Moscow 800. That arrogance was based on physical condition, which was what had been missing the last couple of years. Yet now when I was moderately fit, a couple of domestic meetings had produced tension as debilitating as before the Moscow 800.

The decision Peter and I took in no way changed our relationship. It's important that your coach should be supportive, but tension goes from you to him, and then comes back again from him, emotionally charged. Then it's not a problem halved, it's a problem doubled. A coach is not going to say simply 'forget it, have a beer'. *He's* going to react, too. I've often thought my retirement will in some ways be a greater wrench for Peter and others than for me. That's not to say I don't *need* people. But in June this year I felt I couldn't go on inflicting things on him, hour by hour. Few people realize, outside a handful who've experienced it, the pressures of an Olympics. The three weeks is colossal, it just goes on building up, and I don't think anyone has ever attempted to tackle seven middle-distance races before.

The time gap between losing at Crystal Palace and winning in Oslo was by coincidence about the same as between the two finals in Moscow. Actually *making* the decision we made produced a change in me. I went off to Chicago, after running a minor race for Haringey, with Peter's training routine for the lead up to the Games and the proviso that I had scope for adjustment or modification. It was the pattern we had established over sixteen years. I wasn't going to have a race in America because I didn't think that was the answer. It was the frame of *mind*. After I'd been there a week, working hard in high temperatures, I had the first indication that things were going well, with a series of 20 x 200, the first ten with 25 seconds recovery, the second ten with 35 to 40 seconds recovery. The times were mainly around 26 seconds, but the last one was 22.5, against a personal best ever of 21.7. I'd not been able to produce such quality at the end of a series since 1981. Throughout my career I've never had difficulty running the occasional one-off race with speed, irrespective of training circumstances. That's what screwed me in Athens, I could have perhaps won over two rounds instead of three, or if I hadn't had to run in the relay world record.

In 1983, I could run a 1:43.8 in Oslo even though unwell, but then couldn't string together races later on. This year, I've had even fewer problems than I might have done, no breaks from training apart from that one slight thigh strain. In Chicago, I was getting back into an area of athletic purity, single-mindedness of purpose. The Olympic arena is a very lonely place. Those who get the accolades are those who are at one with themselves. It's a difficult thing to articulate. I was now in a far better frame of mind than six weeks before, when I thought I couldn't win *anything* important this season. Now I felt I had as good a chance as anyone.

For Peter, this was the period that he would later describe as the 'ultimate weaning'. It was all too easy for the outsider, distantly observing his authoritarian manner, to label him proprietory, over-paternal, self-projecting, when he was simply

firm in his convictions and never someone who could suffer fools
lightly. He lets his feelings be known. He himself tells with a
smile the day one of his factory foremen, in the cutlery firm at
Sheffield where he was a director and production manager, said
to him, 'it's not surprising your son can run fast, he probably
does it to get away from a bastard like you'. Yet he was a bastard
of the right sort, whose unflinching priorities were quality,
efficiency and reliability. In the relatively short years that I have
known Peter, I have never been aware of his taking a decision
regarding Seb that had not carefully weighed and measured his
son's interest. The extent of his caring was apparent when he
talked about their mutually agreed time of separation in the
summer of 1984: 'When he went off for five weeks, he had five or
six sheets of paper on which I set out what I wanted him to do.
Seb had gone through it, and agreed with it. It contained all the
old principles we had always worked on, but with a different
mounting rate of intensity, because of the loss of preparation
time. It wasn't based on the certainty of getting to the 800 final
with maximum fitness, but on the old Tour de France maxim of
progressive development through the whole competition, to be
ready to hit them when it hurts. The lifting, or raising, of
intensity included the fitness product from heats and semi-final
races, on the predictable basis that they wouldn't be slow.

'To move at a faster rate than in 1981 was something of a risk,
but I thought he could manage it without harm. It was not just a
matter of being able to use the early races of the Games to
advantage: we *had* to. The contradiction for Seb is that racing will
always be easier than training, and the need is to find a balance
between frequency and intensity. In 1981, we worked on a
progress of endurance leading towards speed, though we never
get down to a point of *only* working on speed. There is always
one long run at the weekend, as in Moscow after the 800 and
again in LA. Our risk now was whether he would have the
endurance to withstand the intensity, and that's why we worked
with only one important race between the AAA and the
Olympics.

'Most people take about eight races to get to a peak. Oslo plus
four races in the 800 in LA, and two heats of the 1,500 made

seven: I worked out he should be ready to defend his title! Because of Seb's recovery rate, he would be able to withstand those first six races in eight days at a high level, getting fitter all the time. The success of coaching lies in tailoring progress to the particular requirements of the individual.

'There is a golden rule: only vary one factor at a time. This year we had to vary two. Firstly, the rate of progression. Secondly, our mutual mental approach. There is a risk of staleness in relationships just as much as in training. What had taken place between Moscow and Los Angeles was that there was a greater difference in Seb between the ages of twenty-four and twenty-eight than there was in me, between sixty and sixty-four. After two disastrous years, I looked back – even with the medical explanations and allowing for everything, I had to be sure no stone was left unturned. In 1984 there was going to be more stress, because of increased intensity, so what could be done to reduce other stress? You might ask why we didn't apply this same attitude to Moscow, but that was a different time, a different place. One learns. Seb has said that it is no use thinking that the Olympics is Zurich or Brussels extended to a fortnight. So much is different. Had he been in the Games in Montreal, when he was nineteen, he probably wouldn't have experienced the lapse in Moscow.

'By common agreement, we recognized that three months had been too long to be training in Rome before the Games in 1980, away from his friends, his music and his studies. We knew he didn't need so much time away now. But off-setting this was the greater difference in time zones between London and western America, so that he needed to be away longer immediately before the Games for acclimatization. I was pushing for it to be longer still, but Seb wanted to keep it the same as we'd planned. The fascinating thing is that I started off knowing more about Seb all those years ago than he did about himself: ultimately, with his accumulated knowledge, he *must* reverse the roles, and know more than I do – so that now I must listen more and more!'

So Seb would go to Oslo on his own, and run superbly, and the disappointed Elliott would go to Brussels and run more than two seconds faster than when beating Coe, but lose by one-hundredth of a second to Verbeeck of Belgium, in an international with England to which Elliott had a commitment but which was doing nothing to help him to prepare for LA. Cram, not wanting to risk further damage to his tendon, withdrew from the international against Spain and Sweden the following Friday on his home track at Gateshead, where his place in the 1,500 metres would be taken by Ovett.

Seb nipped back to London briefly for a quiet outing for Haringey in the Beverley Baxter Trophy. Running inevitably from the front, on a summer evening bathed in sunshine, he recorded the year's then fastest mile with 3:54.6. An article subsequently appeared in a Sunday paper in which Ron Pickering of BBC television, the club president, seemed to claim that joining Haringey had proved to be the making of Seb; that the club had somehow civilized him and brought him down to earth! I don't think they are that much less down to earth in south Yorkshire, where Seb had been training and competing for more than a dozen years. What Seb did appreciate deeply was the altruism he had been shown over the winter months by a handful of local runners who, in the most wretched climatic conditions, had consistently stuck with him in really tough training sessions, taking it in turn to run ahead of him in repetitions, so as to pull out the best in him as he climbed back towards his normal level. As Neil Allen quoted in the London *Standard*:

> They were with me right through the winter, when that hill behind the stadium was a pile of mud, when it was blowing a gale and the snow seemed to be freezing the palms of your hands. Even kids of twelve and thirteen were out there with me. . . . The turning point was when I started to train with the Haringey lads after I came to live in London. You saw me warm up with some of them tonight, they buck you up, they make you laugh. . . . I loved growing up in Yorkshire but, after all, I was born down here, and it has a lot to offer. If I decide to move up to 5,000 metres next season, then it's that same hill I climbed all last winter which will again make some difference.

Seb packed his bags, and his jazz tapes, and headed for Chicago and the home of Joe Newton, a friend of Peter's and a hugely experienced and engaging American coach with a voice which sounds not unlike Jimmy Durante in its infectious enthusiasm. Joe would be good company for someone wanting to concentrate on the brighter side of life. Cram and Ovett would continue with their anxious jockeying of racing fixtures, trying to recover that illusive touch which Seb seemed now to have found. Ovett won a 1,500 metres in Lausanne, withdrew from another in the Talbot Games because of a viral infection which produced a skin rash, and from subsequent meetings in Birmingham, Edinburgh and Oslo, which cast an obvious shadow over his departure for LA. Cram, having pulled up again in a 1,000 metres in the Talbot Games, then recovered moderately with a slow 1,500 in the England international against Poland and Hungary at Birmingham, saying that he still needed two more races to get in shape. Elliott unwisely kept running, and finished eighth in the Oslo 800.

Another defeat for Cram, this time over 1,000 metres in the Edinburgh Games, cut back his morale again, and an injured ankle now added to the problems of his tendon. Jimmy Hedley, his coach, remained optimistic, saying that he was in much the same position as before last year's World Championships. There remained only a date in Oslo for the Dream Mile, but he wisely withdrew from that and opted to rest. 'Steve is in a sort of no man's land, needing races, but knowing they will make the ankle flare up,' said Hedley. 'He is certainly not pulling out of the Olympics, but if it was anybody other than Steve, he'd be as worried as hell at the moment. But apart from his ankle he could not be fitter.' The Olympic Games of 1984 would show that not the least of the qualities of Britain's three competitors in the 1,500 metres was strength of character.

Seven

Playing with Fire

Would there be another Olympic Games after Los Angeles? There were those who believed that these XXIII Olympics would prove to be so bedevilled by political boycott, excessive finance, shameless nationalism, acknowledged professionalism, rampant and undetected drug taking, security against terrorism, inmovable traffic and insufferable smog, that future Games would be in jeopardy. Happily they would be proved wrong, in some instances spectacularly so.

Of course, many of these obstacles will not go away, will remain with us at Seoul and thereafter. Yet the strength of the Olympic movement lies in the fact that it *does* manage to rise above all impediments and that it *will* be here into the next century, always providing the absence of major world disasters. It will survive because of the thousands of competitors who just want to be there, almost anonymously, rather than because of the few hundred who will win medals, even though it is they who create the image of immortal glory. Significantly, an unprecedented number of people had lined city streets and country roads across the breadth of America to catch a glimpse of the controversial but emotive and symbolic torch relay. Months of international argument against this innovation had taken place, lead by the Greeks, whose defence of so-called Olympic purity was undermined when Peter Ueberroth, president of the organizing committee, had revealed that it was the tradition of the Hellenic Olympic Committee to charge the IOC a fat six-figure fee for the four-yearly privilege of lighting the flame in Olympia.

The torch run had generated twelve million dollars charity for youth clubs, from the three thousand dollars donated for each sponsored kilometre run, had given thousands of ordinary people the unique opportunity as runners to be an involved part of an Olympic ceremony, and millions more the memory of being there when the flame passed down *their* street.

A television audience of 2.5 billion watched a record 140 nations march into the Coliseum for the opening ceremony. Ueberroth, the Californian businessman who had master-minded a privately organized and financed event unique in Olympic history, could rightly be proud as he said on the eve of the Games: 'The focus is now where it belongs, on the athletes. The superpowers have learnt that boycotts achieve nothing except hurting the absent athletes.' He and the IOC president, Juan Samaranch, could take satisfaction in staging a record Games on fifty per cent of what was spent by Moscow, thanks in part to 50,000 volunteers in a staff of 72,000. The fact that Seoul, in South Korea, was at this moment ready for the next Olympic Games and that countries were queuing to be hosts in 1992, 1996 and 2000, suggested that the profits of doom, as in religion, may have jumped the gun.

The overriding fear in LA was that some psychopath, such as had recently slaughtered innocent customers – including children – at a McDonalds take-away in San Diego, and another who on the very night of the opening ceremony mowed down pedestrians on the side-walk in a mad frenzy in his car only a quarter of a mile from the UCLA village in Westwood, would blight the show. Yet security made LA currently the best protected city on earth. Overt terrorism seemed impossible: the sky, the streets and roof-tops were crawling with the forces of law, though never oppressively, as in Moscow. As Ueberroth admitted: 'Many thousands of dollars per athlete have been spent, we've given every dime the security organizations wanted, but the threat of terrorism will not be distanced in our lifetime.' Seven thousand men from forty agencies, almost one man per competitor, working three overlapping twelve-hour shifts, were guarding the villages, competition sites and the streets. The FBI had doubled its Californian investigators to 800; President Reagan and heads of states would be protected by 600 guards; and computers could trace any arrested suspect's background in eighteen seconds. Some 1,800 drugs, vice and crime arrests had been made in the three preceding weeks as LA beefed up its vigilance.

Ueberroth denied that the government and state were shouldering hidden costs to the tax payer, and claimed they would make a net profit on taxes of £170 million and £60 million respectively. The post office alone had taken £68 million on Olympic stamps even before the Games began, and millions had been spent in sponsored improvement of permanent sporting facilities – only slightly marred by the story of the workman, absent-mindedly engaged in conversation, who had lowered a massive electronic scoreboard straight through the forum floor at the basketball site. Repairers were busy. Smog and traffic remained imponderable problems. The police were sweating in every sense.

If the opening ceremony was any yardstick by which to measure the next fortnight's sporting festival, we realized we should be grateful and not cynical that a private committee had accepted the daunting burden of the Olympics when the only other candidate city for them, Teheran, failed to come to the line five years before. The United States might carry much of the conscience of the modern world, but now, with a Hollywood zap which suggested friendliness more than vulgarity, Los Angeles welcomed its guests with an open-heartedness and a genuine 'have a nice day'! The three-hour display was often stunningly spectacular, yet never boastful, an exposition of the remarkable kaleidoscope of ethnic races and cultures which have made America great. The cynics might say there was no reference to the genocide of the Red Indians and the shames of slavery. But from the immigrant settlers with their wagons and the dignified, singing negroes emerging from subservience, through to the twentieth-century extravaganza of music, dance and technology it was a pageant in which the overriding theme was of a community with a zest for life and progress, which no smug European should scorn.

The older world, bred on history and tradition, could not remain unmoved when assailed by the 750 trumpets, drums and

trombones of the All American Marching Band playing Prima's
'Sing, Sing, Sing' with an uninhibited exultation which made
one's skin tingle. David Wolper's ceremony was, above all,
memorable for its sense of social justice: when the jet planes had
finished their sky-writing, and the eighty-four grand pianos had
paid glossy tribute to Gershwin; when the thousands of
gymnasts had unleashed the youthful energy which is the voice
of the nation, the bands had played, and the 140 teams had
paraded – with echoing cheers for the communists from
Rumania and China; when the crowd, given no more than a five-
second count-down practice with the announcer, had
unknowingly suddenly produced a canopy of international flags
with the 90,000 individually-held coloured sheets supplied with
their tickets (planned on computer and now upstaging the
carefully-rehearsed Russian display in 1980;) when the huge
American team had made its disordered, extrovert, shambling
entry behind everyone else, and the American president had
fluffed the order of his eighteen-word formal speech, there came
the moment which the world audience awaited. The lighting of
the flame.

Half a century ago Jesse Owens, a poor cotton-family black,
had been obliged to enter stadiums by the side door, even after he
had become the greatest of all Olympians in Berlin. Now, into a
hushed Coliseum, with the sun's sinking rays over the Pacific lip
illuminating the Olympic flag, ran Owens's grand-daughter
Gina Hemphill. Bearing the torch which had wound its way
across 10,000 miles of America, she lapped the track once, side-
stepping competitors with cameras. She passed the torch to Rafer
Johnson, decathlon champion of 1960, who climbed a Busby-
Berkley-style ninety-nine-step staircase beneath the stadium
arches to light the symbolic flame. Owens would have been a
proud man. He would have believed, as I do, that the flame can
still carry its intended meaning of the unity of man. And when
Ed Moses, a third black Olympic champion honoured by the
ceremony, forgot his lines when taking the athletes' oath, it
reminded Americans that we are all ultimately humble.

It was a travesty of the truth to label the Los Angeles Games as
the rip-off games, as some were doing in England and elsewhere.

Of course some of the hotel prices were high, and there *was* initial retail exploitation. The final surprise profit of $150 million, even accepting capacity crowds, is proof of over-charging, though the organizers had to be sure to avoid a loss. Yet in many ways, within the intrinsic Olympic context, it would prove to be an outstanding Games, and nowhere more than in the relaxed environment of the UCLA village, which Sebastian Coe justifiably described as the most enjoyable competing surroundings he had ever experienced, even having attended championships at such places as Prague, Athens, Moscow, Helsinki, and Turin.

Seb was one of the first to arrive in the British quarters, most of the athletics squad having gone first to a training camp near San Diego. What most appealed to Seb, quite apart from the undulating, tree-lined campus, the excellent training track and the more than adequate food, was the extensive medical and physiotherapy facilities. Through the service of volunteer surgeons, almost any major operation could be carried out on the spot, throughout the Games. Elsewhere in the village, facilities were of an extraordinarily high standard. The vast weight-training gymnasium, a positive torture chamber of elaborate modern gadgetry, was superior to anything I have seen, and testimony to the unparalleled finances of American university sport. It was because of the range of facilities available that one of the rumours concerning Seb occurred in the count-down to the start of the 800 metres. Rob Druppers of Holland, silver medallist in Helsinki, had a strain requiring attention, which ultimately forced him to scratch. He noticed that Seb was going in and out of the medical clinic at the same time and drew conclusions. In fact, Seb had been having his eyes tested and collecting new spectacles to replace the ones he had left behind at home.

Another rumour about his fitness, or apparent lack of it, emanated unintentionally from John Walker. On a particular morning Seb had done a severe bout of repetitions. After lunch, he agreed to go on a longish warm-down jog with John, but about half-way found that he was stiffening slightly, and sensibly told the New Zealander that he felt he would be better off paying a visit to the physio. John, unaware of Seb's morning stint, mentioned the incident to a swimming correspondent who happened to be in the village on other work; she mentioned it to the BBC, and within a couple of hours the story had been beamed: 'Coe Injured'.

Other rumours flowing backwards and forwards concerned Said Aouita having to chose between the 1,500 or 5,000 metres, because the timing of the two races conflicted. He was the fastest of the year at both events, and the earlier rumours, coming from San Diego, were that he had opted for 1,500. There were quotes. At least one British paper had him saying: 'When I heard that the finals of the two events were so close that it was impossible to do both, I knew I had to run only the 1,500. It's my event. I know it best, and I want my revenge for Helsinki {where he was third].' Personally, I had my doubts. Aouita must have known that the 5,000 was the softer option and, like Filbert Bayi, who in Moscow had decided to opt out of a fierce 1,500 so as to be sure in the steeplechase of Tanzania's first Olympic medal, he would surely want to guarantee Morocco a medal from the 5,000 – which he could not in the 1,500.

If the count-down was an anxious time for Seb, given the endless tabulation in the public prints of his failures in Prague, Moscow, Athens and, by default, Helsinki, he never showed it. The gold medal in the 800 metres was a passionate ambition for someone who genuinely believed that, for the past five years, no one could touch him when he was at his best. Yet he knew, as few others did, that he was tackling the Olympics as a whole, and that by his own intentional planning – together with Peter – his real peak would arrive, all being well, for the 1,500 final. He had to hope that he would have progressed sufficiently by the time of the 800 final to match anything that anyone else could produce after four races in four days. He was under no illusions. On arrival from Chicago he had told Emery of the *Express*: 'It's going to be a cut-throat two weeks. Some of the races will be savage. There will be powerful racing rather than some of the scruffy tactical battles we have seen before. I'm ready for it, I'm feeling good.'

Certainly that was how it seemed to me when I met him

several times, either in the village or for a relaxing meal down at Santa Monica on Ocean Boulevard, overlooking the miles of golden sands which stretch farther than the eye can see – northwards to Malibu and south to Long Beach, Newport Beach and all the way to San Diego. Tanned and lean, with that slightly gaunt look he has when supremely conditioned, I was conscious that it was a changed athlete I was talking to. However tough it was going to be, he was ready for it, and anything but nervous. He was benefitting from having come early to America to acclimatize to the time difference and the high temperatures, though the latter is something which never bothers him. He likes the heat, and I sensed that he was looking forward to the confrontation with the four men, Jones, Gray, Cruz and Sabia, whose recent times suggested that this would be one of the toughest events of the Games.

Jones, from Michigan University, just twenty, had been winding up everyone's expectations with some provocative comments. In a widely reported interview he said:

> I'm improving every time I run. Out of the British, I think Coe is the best, but whether he can take four races in such a short time we will have to wait and see. I know *I* can, because I went through it in the US trials. I was not at my peak then, but I will be next week. I don't want it slow, and I'm prepared to run from the front if necessary, but I'm prepared to conserve my energy until the others show me what they have got.

In the trials he and Gray shared the US record of 1:43.74, though Joaquim Cruz of Brazil, with a personal best for the year of 1:44.04, had beaten Jones during the season.

The tall Cruz, twenty-one, seemed more the man to fear. He was the son of a poor carpenter in a near-slum suburb of Brazilia. Since the age of eleven and a half he had been coached by Luiz Alberto Oliveira, whom he had met at a sports club where Oliveira was involved with basketball and athletics. Young Cruz's ambitions had been as much in basketball as in athletics – which in Brazil hardly rated as a sport alongside soccer and basketball. For the next four years he played anything and everything under the shrewd eye of Oliveira, who would became as much a friend as coach. 'It was not until he was sixteen that I really encouraged him to work at his running, so that he would not become addicted to the more normal passions of ball games,' says Oliveira, fourteen years senior to this outstanding athlete who has a build so reminiscent of the Montreal double champion, Juantorena – 'The Horse'. Oliveira told me:

'Joaquim hated running, and he had no help of any sort in the early days. No spikes. At sixteen he ran his first 1,500 metres in 4:18. Then we found him some spikes, and immediately he reduced that by twelve seconds. Through the knowledge of my job, I tried to pay careful attention to his growth physiology, and by the time he was eighteen he set a world junior record of 1:44.3 for the 800. It was after that he was selected to run in the World Cup in Rome in 1981, but nobody knew he had an ankle injury and was unable to train for fifteen days beforehand.' It was in 1981 that Cruz's father died. Brigham Young University in Utah invited Cruz and Oliveira to the States; in 1983 they switched to the University of Oregon, where Oliveira, supported by Nike, settled with his family. Cruz's development continued, and this year he had become the national universities' champion at both 800 and 1,500, both of which he planned to attack in the coming fortnight.

Peter Elliott, whose courageous front running had probably cost Cruz the gold or silver in Helsinki, was busy denying that he had an injury which could have been seen as an excuse for his poor performance in his last run in Oslo before departure for LA. He told Christopher Hilton of the *Express*: 'There is no truth in that, and there is nothing wrong with me. I had lost my racing edge. It was my first 800 since I qualified for the Olympics [why?] and it worried me a lot. I put it down to being race rusty.' Elliott had run some of the worry out of his system by winning a 1,500 metres in San Diego against a field including Steve Scott; but he increased the speculation about his condition when he admitted to Emery that he had had some trouble with bruising around his instep which had been cleared up by a cortisone injection. The twenty-two-year-old was bravely talking now about a gold medal.

Ovett, the defending champion, was voicing similar optimism and talking of being capable of running 1:43. Yet he had never run that in his life, and his fastest ever time was 1:44.01 six years ago. He would be hard pressed to get near that, given his present background. On the day of the first round, the rankings for the year were:

1:43.74 – Jones and Gray (USA); 1:43.84 – Coe; 1:43.88 – Sabia (Italy); 1:43.92 – Marshall (USA); 1:44.60 – Guimaraes (Brazil); 1:45.10 – Cruz; 1:45.17 – Koskei (Kenya); 1:45.20 – Konchellah (Kenya); 1:45.45 – Ferner (West Germany); 1:45.56 – Fall (Senegal); 1:45.60 – Gilbert (Australia); 1:45.62 – Braun (West Germany); 1:45.72 – Elliott; 1:45.75 – Mayr (Switzerland); 1:45.78 – Khalifa (Sudan); 1:45.81 – Trabado (Spain); 1:45.83 – Assmann (West Germany); 1:45.90 – Pearless (NZ) and Scammell (Australia); 1:46.15 – Ovett

At 6.45 in the evening, the stadium was no more than half full on the first day of track and field. In the first heat of Round One, Sabia was third, a shade outside 1:47. What became apparent, in the very first of four rounds, was the fierce quality of the event. No less than fourteen runners ran under 1:47, whereas in Moscow, where there were only three rounds, none broke 1:47 in the heats and only six did in the semi-finals. In heat two, Coe became one of three to go under 1:46 in the first round, the others being Khalifa and Cruz. As Coe jogged in a final warm-up on the yellow run-up of the high jump area, sky-writing jets overhead were tracing out 'US – Go for Gold'. The sun burned down, and much of the green colouring dye on the in-field from the opening ceremony had now faded, leaving the grass a bronzed olive. Coe waved to a few Brits in the crowd, had a quick spit to clear his mouth, and they were off – after a false start when several runners had a foot over the line. The pace was brisk: Materazzi of Italy led at the bell in 52.30, Coe accelerated round the third bend, took over the lead coming off the fourth, and with repeated glances and minor spurts ran comfortably to the line to find he had a time of 1:45.71, with Khalifa only a tenth of a second slower.

Jones, in heat four, had a relatively gentle run with 1:47.75, but in the next, Cruz, though clearly coasting in some way ahead of Ovett, recorded a warning 1:45.66. Heat six produced a real race.

With only the first three certain to qualify for the second round, which would include the next five fastest overall, Gray led at the second bend, Belkessam of Algeria was second at the bell (52.43), with Scammell of Australia coming through to take up third down the back straight. There was a battle down the final 70 metres, with Mayr of Switzerland coming through to take third place behind Gray and Scammell, all of them inside 1:47.50. Koech, Ferner and Guimaraes all had to look sharp to finish in the front three in heat seven. Elliott, looking conspicuously pale in an otherwise all black ninth heat, was fourth at the lane break, led at the bell in 51.86, was passed on the third bend by Konchellah and Barbosa of Brazil, but came back to take second with 1:46.98 behind the strolling Konchellah.

'It's a bit quick for the heats,' said Seb afterwards. 'They're pretty brisk out there, because there are some guys going out with a do-or-die attitude in the first lap and then not even qualifying. Whether it's too fast or not we'll know at the end of four days. Perhaps it is, but it's the same for everybody. The semi-finals are going to be tough. It's nice to get back into competition, which is better than the daily grind of training. A peak? It's too early to tell, but I'm in good shape, for my race felt slower than it turned out to be.'

Round Two was no less remarkable than the first, with fourteen men going under 1:46, of whom three failed to qualify: Lahbi of Morocco, Niang of Senegal and Alouini of Tunisia. Elliott found himself in the first and fastest heat of the four, with four qualifying places in each. Koech, who had led from gun to tape in his first round heat, did so again. He was followed down the first back straight by Sabia and Elliott, with Niang straining to stay with them. Into the second straight, Elliott moved up behind Koech, the pair of them passing the 400 in around 51.3, with Niang and Sabia third and fourth. The order remained the same down the back straight, and Elliott was still close on Koech entering the last 100 metres. Here Sabia went wide past Elliott, who was fading, and Guimaraes went by on the inside. Elliott held on to fourth, a fraction ahead of Lahbi, who had left it too late, and Niang, who was sixth. A ninety thousand crowd roared their approval. Koech and Sabia both ran under 1:45.

As Coe warmed up before the second heat, there was a spatter of applause as the loudspeakers announced that he was the world record holder. (Up to now, little had been done by the announcer to educate the crowd in the real relevance of what they were watching. Most of them had spent forty or sixty dollars because it was the Olympics; many of them were probably watching track and field for the first time.) Belkessam led for a lap and a half, going through the bell in 51.41. Coe was fifth or sixth at the bell, and only made his move after a jumble coming off the third bend, in which he all but fell, had cleared itself. Down the back straight Konchellah moved ahead of Marshall, and came off the last bend ahead of Khalifa and Coe. Marshall began to fade badly and lost the fourth qualifying place to Barbosa. It turned out to be the slowest of the four heats, with Coe six tenths down on Konchellah's winning 1:46.15.

Cruz and Gray were first and second most of the way in the third heat, Cruz always in control. Ovett was third at the bell, which Cruz passed in 51.26, and down the third straight Ovett was six yards down on Cruz and two on Gray. Cruz, with two glances back on the final bend, won as he pleased by a distance in 1:44.84, while Ovett, with a season's best of 1:45.72, pipped Gray for second. Ndiwa of Kenya made the running in heat four, pursued by Jones and Ferner. Jones led after 600 to win by a couple of strides from Ferner in 1:45.44.

Peter's opinion was that the series would go on getting faster. 'I think the final will depend on attitude of mind on the day, who goes to the line feeling right. Cruz is obviously running with great confidence, and it seems certain that in the final we shall have a very fast first 600, in around 75 seconds, with someone then hanging on for around 27, 28. It will probably need 1:43 to win, with the Olympic record going. There were obviously people out there today who can go under that time. I don't think for the moment, on today's evidence, we should write off Ovett. You can't easily throw off a man who has recently run a 3:34 for a 1,500. If he survives the semi-final, and he's still in contact in a tactical race in the final, he should still be able to produce a kick. I get the impression that Gray may be better than Jones but there's not a lot between them. We should also remember that Seb ran such an easy 1:43.8 in Oslo.' What Peter had no way of knowing was the breathing difficulty which Ovett was experiencing, which would manifest itself the next day.

800 metres Round Two Splits

Heat 1 200	24.52 Sabia (Italy)		*Heat 2* 200	24.86 Belkessam (Algeria)	
400	51.29 Elliott (GB)		400	51.41 Belkessam (Algeria)	
	51.29 Koech (Kenya)			51.54 Mayr (Switzerland)	
	51.45 Niang (Senegal)			51.66 Khalifa (Sudan)	
	51.50 Sabia (Italy)			51.77 Marshall (USA)	
	51.66 Giumaraes (Brazil)			51.86 Materazzi (Italy)	
	51.70 Lahbi (Morocco)			51.93 Coe (GB)	
	51.87 Moutsanas (Greece)			52.11 Konchellah (Kenya)	
600	1:18.30 Koech (Kenya)			52.18 Barbosa (Brazil)	
800	1:44.74 Koech (Kenya)		600	1:19.70 Belkessam (Algeria)	
			800	1:46.15 Konchellah (Kenya)	
Heat 3 200	24.57 Cruz (Brazil)		*Heat 4* 200	24.90 Ndiwa (Kenya)	
400	51.25 Cruz (Brazil)		400	50.89 Ndiwa (Kenya)	
	51.63 Gray (USA)			50.94 Jones (USA)	
	51.78 Ovett (GB)			51.09 Alouini (Tunisia)	
	51.80 Bile (Somalia)			51.10 Ferner (West Germany)	
	52.01 Wuyke (Venezuela)			51.27 Fall (Senegal)	
	52.14 Roberts (Canada)			51.32 Barr (Guyana)	
	52.19 Hamilton (Jamaica)			51.61 O'Sullivan (Ireland)	
	52.40 Scammell (Australia)			51.90 DuPont (France)	
600	1:18.08 Cruz (Brazil)		600	1:18.16 Jones (USA)	
800	1:44.84 Cruz (Brazil)		800	1:45.44 Jones (USA)	

Faster and faster they continued. Nothing could have illustrated the mood more than the fact that Cruz went off from the gun in the first semi-final, in lane 2 between Ovett and Koech, and covered the first 100 in 12.17 seconds, with Koech and Jones (lane 8) yielding little ground. Jones then took over the lead from the lane break, and covered the back straight in an astonishing 11.52 for a 200 time of 23.69 as they entered the second bend; Cruz and Koech were close behind him, with Khalifa running wide in lane 2, then Ovett, Fall of Senegal and Wuycke of Venezuela in a group. Some twelve yards covered the distance between Jones and Wuyke, and Ovett's bid to stay with such pace was taking an inner toll.

Round the second bend Khalifa moved past Koech, and entering the second straight the order was Jones – Cruz – Khalifa

– Koech, with Ovett coming up wide, presumably with the intention of being placed to go with anyone who broke after the bell. In the twenty to thirty yards before the bell, Koech went past the front three to lead in a fierce 49.56, Ovett going through fifth in 50.4. Round the third bend Cruz overtook Jones but was still two yards down on Koech; Ovett, hands dropping slightly, was battling to stay in touch for a qualifying place in a private battle with Fall and Khalifa.

Koech held his lead for some 300 metres after the bell but could not resist Cruz, who kicked coming into the finishing straight. On the crown of the last bend Ovett had attacked on the outside of Jones (third), failed, and fell back to fifth. Down the finishing straight, Jones, who had been boxed behind Cruz and Khalifa on the back straight, now surged through on the inside of Khalifa, who still had a yard and a half on Ovett.

Coming towards the line, Ovett made a desperate bid for fourth place: his head and shoulders rolling, he literally threw himself across the line to make it by six-hundredths of a second. He fell to his hands and knees, and was clearly in distress after the fastest time he had run (1:44.81) since the Prague European Championships. Khalifa, former colleague of Seb's at Loughborough, had set a Sudan record, yet was out. With 1:43.82, Cruz had set a South American record.

Elliott had scratched from the semi-final. A brief test in the village in the morning had shown that the arch under his instep was too painful even to begin to sprint. The story began to emerge that he had been living with this problem for some months – which certainly meant that it had been ill-advised of him to have indulged in four-lap races after he had missed 1,500-metres selection, and calling into question Paish's argument that his athlete should contest two events rather than one.

Jones, third behind Koech, said afterwards: 'I was not worried with 200 to go, even though I was boxed. I knew this would break up coming off the bend, so I relaxed and waited. I was just trying to make the top four today. The real running will take place tomorrow. I'm not concerned with the time tomorrow, just the gold medal.'

Seb's face seemed taut to me before the second semi-final, but it was probably concentration. Gray was off fast in lane 4, but coming out of the lane-break it was Coe, Barbosa and Ndiwa, the three inside lane men, who were in line. By the second bend, Gray had gone in front, ahead of a bunched group including Coe, Ferner, Konchellah and Guimaraes. Into the second straight Gray led from Konchellah, who had Sabia at his shoulder; Coe was running wide in lane 2, Ferner fifth behind him in lane 1. Gray passed the bell in 52.3, Coe in 52.5, fourth together with Ferner. Into the last bend it was Gray and Konchellah, with Coe poised in third position, running wide, and Sabia and Ferner tracking him. Half-way through the bend Coe pounced, opening a lead which he sustained easily, while behind him Konchellah, Gray, Sabia and Ferner fanned out just ahead of Guimaraes – five fighting for three qualifying places. Twenty metres out, Sabia raised his pace to take fourth, as Ferner and Guimaraes faded. Gray, third in 1:45.82, said afterwards: 'I took a real close look at Seb as he went past, and though to myself that I'm not going to mess about with him today.' Konchellah, second, seemed unduly optimistic about the final: 'Maybe Coe. Maybe me.' As Peter had said, you have to believe in yourself in this game.

800 metres Semi-final Splits

Heat 1			Heat 2		
100	12.17 Cruz (Brazil)		100	12.25 Barbosa (Brazil)	
200	23.69 Jones (USA)		200	24.63 Konchellah (Kenya)	
300	36.32 Jones (USA)		300	38.06 Gray (USA)	
400	49.56 Koech (Kenya)		400	52.26 Gray (USA)	
	49.61 Jones (USA)			52.34 Sabia (Italy)	
	49.79 Cruz (Brazil)			52.41 Konchellah (Kenya)	
	49.95 Khalifa (Sudan)			52.51 Coe (GB)	
	50.38 Ovett (GB)			52.55 Ferner (West Germany)	
	50.50 Fall (Senegal)			52.66 Guimaraes (Brazil)	
	51.52 Wuyke (Venezuela)			52.85 Barbosa (Brazil)	
				52.88 Ndiwa (Kenya)	
500	1:03.09 Koech (Kenya)		500	1:05.93 Gray (USA)	
600	1:16.88 Koech (Kenya)		600	1:19.30 Gray (USA)	
700	1:29.98 Cruz (Brazil)		700	1:32.00 Coe (GB)	
800	1:43.82 Cruz (Brazil)		800	1:45.51 Coe (GB)	

I drove Seb and Peter back to the village, before returning with Peter to downtown LA, where he caught his regular bus back to his friends' house in Long Beach. The two of them had not talked

that much on the journey down the Santa Monica–San Diego
freeway to Westwood. There was not really that much to say.
They had met a couple of times in the village before the racing
began, done a few repetitions, had a quiet lunch. All was well.
Each of them knew that the pattern they had devised was taking
shape. Now it was up to Seb. Each of them was relaxed, Peter
quite without the concern or Seb the anxiety which had afflicted
them in Moscow. Seb was getting back to the village for a
massage, dinner and an early night; it could have been just
another evening in Loughborough or Sheffield or London.

It was only after we had dropped Seb off that Peter began to
think more about something that was bothering him slightly. He
had got wind of the fact that Gray might be going to try to
surprise the field over the first lap, whereas Seb's opinion was
that the man to track would be Cruz. Peter was concerned that
Seb should not be lulled into the trap of following the wrong man
and allowing anyone else to get a jump of a vital three or four
metres in mid-race, or to separate him from the front pace – as in
Moscow. So before he caught his bus, we went over to the
Biltmore Hotel to the IOC press centre, and put a message on the
computer system which Seb would be able privately to 'key'
open with his personal identification number the next morning
in the village – one of the technological masterpieces of the
Games in LA, which any accredited competitor, official and
journalist could use. Peter's message was:

> Dear Seb. Great run today. You will run your own race tomorrow. I
> only want to make one observation. If when think that a 48.5 start is
> mad and that 49.5 is better, remember that one second is worth eight
> metres, or over twenty-six feet, or three and a half strides. When
> going that fast, any gap could let in another runner fighting for the
> lead and spoil your essential contact. As we know from the past, it's
> seldom a two horse race, and I've found that Gray thinks he is in with
> a good chance. Just a thought from the old coach. With love. I know
> you can.

Mid-race in the 800m final, as Coe latches on to Joachim Cruz (093) and they both overtake Earl Jones of America (909). Steve Ovett seems to be in contention, but his bronchitis sapped his strength to leave him in last place at the finish – he had collapsed at the end of the semi-final the previous day, having had breathing problems for several weeks *(Associated Press Ltd)*

Opposite: Cruz, his huge stride and six years advantage too much for Coe (359), raises his arm in triumph at the first ever gold medal on the track for Brazil, and at a new Olympic record of 1:43.00: a time only Coe has ever beaten. Third was Earl Jones (USA) (909), fourth Billy Konchella (Kenya) (885) and fifth Donato Sabia (Italy) (behind Jones) *(Ian Stewart/Times)*

The end of an era. Coe, with a second consecutive 800m silver, and Ovett, 1980 gold medalist and now last to finish, commiserate with each other (above). 'We're too old to be playing with fire,' says Coe. On the medal rostrum behind Cruz (left), he reflects that he will now never fulfil his ambition of a major 800m gold medal
(Both photos: Ian Stewart/Times)

Steve Ovett looks back at the prostrate
Pierre Deleze of Switzerland, a potential
medalist, who has tripped on Ovett's heel
a few yards from the line in the 1,500m
heats, and is eliminated
(Associated Press Ltd)

A study in concentration among the
crowded field of twelve on the first lap of
the 1,500m final. From right: Chesire
(578), Khalifa (780), Scott, Coe, Vera,
Cram, Abascal (hidden), Materazzi (508),
Rogers, Spivey, Ovett (388) and,
unseen, Wirtz
(Ian Stewart/Times)

Coming off the final bend Coe makes his third kick which Cram, beginning to roll, cannot match. Abascal (219) was third. Coe's perfect rhythm carries him to an Olympic record of 3:32.53 and a come-back without parallel *(Ian Stewart/Times)*

Two faces of victory: joy (above) and revenge (left) as Coe becomes the first man in almost eighty years to win consecutive gold medals in the 1,500m. His face of defiance was directed at those press and television commentators who a year before had written off his chances of ever returning to the top
(Top: Popperfoto. Bottom: Ian Stewart/Times)

Opposite: Princess Anne, president of the British Olympic Association, congratulates Coe at the track-side (inset) following his lap of honour on one of the few occasions when the 98,000 Coliseum crowd had to cheer a visitor
(Ian Stewart/Times. Inset: Popperfoto)

The smiling double champion can relax, after more than two years of anguish and disappointment, with a victory few had believed possible. Steve Cram, the European, Commonwealth and World Champion, accepts the silver medal, with some gracious post-race tributes to the winner. Would both of them now move up to challenge the 5,000m gold medalist, Aouita of Morocco? *(Associated Press Ltd)*

The draw for the final in lane order was:

1 Earl Jones (USA)
2 Donato Sabia (Italy)
3 Sebastian Coe (GB)
4 Billy Konchellah (Kenya)
5 Johnny Gray (USA)
6 Joaquim Cruz (Brazil)
7 Steve Ovett (GB)
8 Edwin Koech (Kenya)

As the runners gathered at the starting line, the hammer event was taking place. Overhead, the Goodyear inflatable airship circled its advertisement continuously. The Olympic flag billowed lightly in a gentle evening breeze, with the floodlights taking over from the sunset. I felt sorry for Ovett. At lunch-time I had been asked by some friends, who were toying with the idea of placing money on him, where I thought he would finish, to which I had said I felt it was less a question of 'where' than 'whether'. On the evidence of his semi-final, it seemed that he had only two choices: to come in at the back of a talented and younger field, or try to contest a place and blow up because of his breathing restrictions.

In the first fifty metres or so it seemed that Jones, on the inside, was up on Sabia and fractionally on Coe; out of the lane-break it was Koech and Cruz leading from Jones, with Ovett fourth, a position he held going into the second bend ahead of Coe, Sabia, Gray and Konchellah, nine-tenths of a second covering the field. In the next 200 metres that span closed to six-tenths, as the field became more bunched. Coming off the second bend, Koech was running freely in the middle of the inside lane, with Cruz at his right shoulder and Jones hugging the kerb. Ovett was in line behind Cruz, with Coe running wide just into lane 2, ahead of Konchellah and Sabia. Down the straight Coe went past Ovett to be third at the bell in 51.3, two-tenths down on Koech and just over one-tenth behind Cruz. Jones was still on the kerb almost level with Coe.

Coe was sticking to his plan of shadowing Cruz, convinced

that the enormously powerful young Brazilian was the man to beat. Koech held his advantage to the 600 mark, and was digging in round the final bend, trying to sustain what was now only a fractional lead. On the peak of the bend Cruz struck: Koech was not to know for another twenty strides that three more would go past him in Cruz's wake. At the very moment Cruz kicked, so did Coe, a stride behind. Coe's kick pulled him fractionally away from Jones, who was moving wide to clear Koech, with Konchellah making a late burst too, from fifth or sixth. Ovett's bid had died at the end of the back straight, and Gray was also way out of touch and any hope of a medal.

Off the bend and into the straight, Coe glanced inside, but the only danger to him was out there in front, that towering bronze figure who was pulling away. One moment, on the final curve of the last bend, there were five almost in a group. Soon there were three strung out. For a few strides it had seemed Coe might hold his young rival but, as he would admit later, the gold was won and lost between 130 and 70 metres out.

As they entered the home straight Coe and Jones, almost side by side, had a minor contact and there was a momentary, fleeting break of rhythm. With Cruz two and a half metres clear, Coe and Jones went past Koech, who was fading quickly; and now Cruz was three and a half metres clear. Thirty yards out, the last despairing ebb of Coe's kick edged him away from Jones; and Cruz was four and a half metres clear. Konchellah's late run, and a surge by Sabia, gave them fourth and fifth places in front of the drained Koech. Way back was Gray, and then the distant Ovett.

The fact that Coe had run much of the second and fourth bends wide in lane two, for tactical freedom to be able to react to Cruz, may have robbed him of more than a stride advantage over Jones, but it could never have made that final difference of between four and five metres behind Cruz, who had lowered the Olympic record to 1:43.00. None could deny that Cruz was the man of the moment, the first Brazilian ever to win an Olympic track title. The inexorable march of time, the persistance of youth coming up over the horizon, spares no athletic champion. If the silver medal for Coe was a personally gratifying triumph over adversity, the gold medal of Cruz symbolized the fuel of the Olympic flame: the fire burns endlessly, new era after new era.

'The message is fairly clear now,' a respectful Seb observed with a smile afterwards. It was the conclusion of his career in his strongest passion – the middle-distance race which through his example, set over the past five years, has become the longest of sustained sprints. 'I'm half delighted to have won a silver after a year of anxieties and restricted preparation, half disappointed that I shall never now have that major championship gold medal. Now I shall go for the more appropriate distance, the 5,000.' Cruz was the supreme champion, said Seb, with a generosity which impressed Americans, and disarmed those who had said he could not take defeat in Moscow.

All of Brazil was suddenly celebrating the gold medal of the new champion most of them had never heard of. He said he would be happier if his gold medal was recognized back home not by celebrations and receptions but by the building of a track. It had been the first of the four races in which he had not run from the front. 'I knew the pace was going to be hard,' he said, 'so I cruised at the first 200 to see if anyone else would take the lead. The guy from Kenya pushed ahead, he did what I always wanted someone to do, so that I could save myself for a kick over the last 150. I'd thought about the possibility of breaking 1:43, but I lost a little energy in the earlier races, so I'm really glad with the Olympic record today. Maybe the world record can be broken in a single race.'

After the finish of the race Seb had walked several yards arm in arm in mutual commiseration with his old adversary, the fallen 1980 gold medallist. 'We're too old to be playing with such fire,' Seb had said to Steve. They had come a long way side by side, if not exactly always together! It was a sad close to Ovett's two-lap running in three consecutive Olympics – he was fifth behind Juantorena's world record in Montreal – and soon after his few words with Seb, he was overcome in the tunnel by chest pains and hyperventilation, and was rushed to the LA orthopaedic hospital where he was fed intravenously. His participation in the 1,500 metres, due to begin two days later, was in the gravest doubt.

800 metres Final Splits

200			400		
	24.02	Koech (Kenya)		51.07	Koech
	24.15	Cruz (Brazil)		51.16	Cruz
	24.24	Jones (USA)		51.29	Coe
	24.38	Ovett (GB)		51.30	Jones
	24.52	Coe (GB)		51.32	Gray
	24.72	Sabia (Italy)		51.45	Ovett
	24.79	Gray (USA)		51.58	Sabia
	24.90	Konchellah (Kenya)		51.64	Konchellah
600	1:17.80	Koech	800	1:43.00	Cruz
	1:17.83	Cruz		1:43.64	Coe
	1:17.93	Coe		1:43.83	Jones
	1:17.98	Konchellah		1:44.03	Konchellah
	1:17.99	Jones		1:44.53	Sabia
	1:18.23	Gray		1:44.86	Koech
	1:18.33	Sabia		1:47.89	Gray
	1:18.53	Ovett		1:52.28	Ovett

Eight

Who says I'm Finished!

The odd thing about Los Angeles is that, in a sense, it does not really exist. Or rather nobody actually lives, as they say, 'downtown'. Anybody I met during the month I was there always lived miles away, in Long Beach or Santa Monica or Pasadena or Burbank. That is why they need all those ten-lane freeways. Eighteen villages in search of a city, said W.C. Fields.

New Yorkers, who think they have the best of all cosmopolitan cultures, dismissively say that the only way people in LA ever meet is when they crash. It is impossible to ask the way if you get lost in your car, especially in the smart suburbs, because there are no pedestrians. Everyone is on wheels. For the journalists, stuck downtown in a sombre, over-charging hotel called the Mayflower (and almost as old), which was due to be demolished a few days after we checked out if it did not fall down first, it was like covering a football tournament at Wembley based in a hotel in Threadneedle Street. There is nobody around after five, they have all come down out of the handful of skyscraper banks and insurance buildings – I think Croydon has more skyscrapers than LA – and motored over to Long Beach, leaving their smog behind.

Fortunately, against all predictions, the Games seemed to have frightened away half the commuters. The freeways were running smoothly and, although some parking lots near the Coliseum began by asking fifty dollars, after a few days it was easy to find a nearby space for five. Attendance at all sports had been a near sell-out, though hotels, car-hire firms and retail businesses reported no surge, and cinemas were saying they were half empty. Downtown stores were already selling Olympic

117

souvenirs at half price inside the first week. For some of those
looking for early retirement in Hawaii, the Games were a let down.

What *did* distinguish the Games was the friendliness. I did not
encounter a single discourteous or aggressive person the whole
time I was there, though I'd been expecting it to be like those
terrible late evening TV films we are shown, with an endless
screaming of tyres, smashing of windows and people being
thrown full-length over boardroom tables or down flights of
stairs. Of course, the enforcement agencies had in recent weeks
arrested most of the pimps, hookers and muggers in a sanitary
scouring, and there were now almost as many police about as
there were traffic lights, and more than there had been, quite
needlessly, in Moscow four years before, yet they were never
offensive. Now, I kept on being smiled at by total strangers.
Perhaps it was some campaign to be nice to the visitors which
disintegrated after we left, but the feeling was that Californians
are a good bunch, providing they have the price of the rent.

The Mexican running a parking lot insisted on introducing me
to his wife, who was cleaning their car. A black security lady
searching hand baggage at the Coliseum sweetly said she hoped
that she had not caused me any inconvenience. The staff at all the
stadia were a lesson in graciousness to those too often surly
individuals selling over-priced inferior food grudgingly with
disinterest at British sports events. I had been gratuitously and
humourously chatted up by garbage collectors asking for
souvenir pins, lady bus drivers, traffic policemen, even when I
nearly went over their polished toe caps, school children, shoe
salesmen, and dozens of the 50,000 assistants who were giving
their services free, and without whom the show would have
collapsed. Ueberroth had said in February that what Sarajevo
had at the Winter Olympics and LA did not, was massive public
goodwill. He was proved wrong.

Television was the real bad news. The domestic coverage by
ABC was almost laughably chauvinistic, even by Italian,
Australian or British standards, and the presenters and
interviewers were persistently ignorant on background,
inaccurate on fact, and inarticulate or over-emotional or both.
Almost no one was shown but American competitors.

Reporting the 20-kilometre walk, we were told that two Mexicans came first and second in the 'run', but not who was third. The interview was with the silver medallist because he was American-Mexican. The announcer said he was a favourite in the 50-kilometre walk, 'which takes places sometime next week, I think'. When Nawal El Moutawakel, the first ever African or Arabic, never mind Moroccan, woman to win a gold medal, was busy giving her answers in English at the press interview, these being translated back into Arabic or French for the benefit of the North African journalists, an American TV commentator suddenly halted the interpreter by shouting: 'Hold on a minute! Do we have to have these interruptions?' Someone politely pointed out that the Games were international, not American, and the lady's language was French or Arabic, not English, which she was speaking out of courtesy to his ignorance.

Some of the more sensitive Americans regularly apologized for the myopia of their television coverage. In the most professional Olympics ever, ABC had paid $225 million and therefore, I suppose, had the right to make as ass of itself. Technically the coverage was superb, but no wonder the IOC president protested about the content.

One man hoping not to make an ass of himself was Steve Cram. The last few weeks of his preparation in Europe before leaving for LA had been a succession of problems, and he only became convinced that it was worth his getting on the plane after he had run a private time trial, among club colleagues in the north east, in a respectable 3:39.8. Among those he had beaten were the experienced Rob Harrison and young Ikem Billy, and for the first time in several races he had finished without discomfort. The tendon and ankle were mending. As Jimmy Hedley said, there was no reason why, with the sun on his back and the stimulation of big crowds, he should not be able to produce the sort of times which would add the Olympic title to his European, Commonwealth and World medals.

The prospects in the last few days for the 1,500 metres had been clarified by the decision of Aouita, no doubt with the same reasoning by Walker, to go for the 5,000 metres. The speculation now centred on whether Cruz and Coe could maintain their

effort with only two days rest following the 800; whether Cram
was fully fit; and whether Ovett would accept the diagnosis of
American doctors that he was not too unwell to run, and would
go against the advice of his own team managers, of his wife and
the British doctors, who all said it was inadvisable. And of
course, the Americans were busy talking about Steve Scott and
Jim Spivey.

The day after Cruz's gold medal, Cram gave a press
conference in the main press centre, which had quite the best
working lay-out and organization that I have encountered at a
major games. The tall, slim Geordie, the most unassuming of
world champions, said that he did not think he would need to be
in shape to run a world record in Saturday's final, 'but I'll have to
be able to run a very fast last lap'. He admitted he would not
know until he stepped off the track after Thursday's first round
just how much the injuries of the last seven weeks had taken out
of him, and he admitted, too, the arrival of an exceptional new
opponent . . . Cruz. 'That was a brilliant performance [in the 800
metres]. Cruz ran faster and faster each day. If I ran four races like
that I wouldn't be able to stand up,' he said with that self-effacing
humour which never allows him to be too serious. 'The problem
with Cruz will be that he has the choice either to lead in the final,
or to wait and then kick. With most of the other runners, I have
an idea how to plan against them, but I've never raced against
Cruz and it will be difficult. Mind you, I wonder if he knows
what he's in for. He may not know the effect of what the 800 has
taken out of him till he hits the bell on Saturday, and finds out
what's left.'

Always a realist, Cram tried to keep the Olympics in
perspective, not to accept that his entire career might be judged
on his performance here, irrespective of his other
accomplishments. 'You've got to try to treat the Olympics like
any other race, not let it seem bigger. You don't want to be
frightened; of course you must be emotionally *up* for it, but I'll
probably race the same guys in Zurich the next week. If I get
beaten, I won't lie down and accept that the guy who won is
number one.' Someone asked him if he'd had any trouble with
his breathing because of the smog. 'If you lived where I live with

all that hydrogen sulphide in the air,' he joked, 'you wouldn't be bothered by this.'

His situation now was a bit different, he thought, compared with Helsinki last year, though each time he had arrived unsure of his fitness. Last year he had missed ten weeks before the start of the season, and had been getting fit late, on races. This season, he had not missed any preparation but had lost the speed-sharpening races close to the Games. His frame of mind was much the same. 'Some people think I'll win on one leg, but I'll just be pleased as long as I finish well, doing the best I can on the day, like Seb did yesterday.'

In the days leading up to the 1,500 metres, Steve Scott from Arizona, for so long in the shadow of one or other of Britain's string of outstanding runners, was permitting himself more optimism than was perhaps discreet, considering that he had had anything but an outstanding year so far, and was only twelfth on the ranking list. None could deny that Scott, twenty-eight, had for a long time been a formidable competitor. Quite apart from his silver behind Cram in Helsinki, and his mile defeat of an ailing Coe last year, in 1982 he had run a mile in Oslo in 3:47.69, not much more than a stride outside Coe's world record of the previous summer. A talented golfer and recreational javelin thrower, he had come into athletics as a former baseball pitcher. Discussing the prospects now, he had been somewhat disparaging about the British, saying that the rest of the world had caught up with British milers. 'Hardly anyone is thinking about Coe and Ovett any more. They're just faces in the crowd. Any one of eight finalists could win the 1,500,' Scott had said after running a modest 800 at Walnut, thirty milers east of Los Angeles, just before the Games began.

Scott is a nice man, and it is difficult to take offence at any opinion he might express, because it would be sincere. It had been Scott from whom Seb ran away 500 metres from the finish when he first broke the mile record in 1979. Now his coach, Len Miller, was also full of optimism during the count-down. He was saying: 'All Steve can do is get hurt, or over work. He's about one hundred per cent ready, and I'm just keeping him sharp with a few daily 200s.' For the first time Scott had the

British on home ground: would he be able to exploit it? In an interview with *Track and Field News*, Miller had once said:

> There isn't any single factor that is most outstanding about Steve except what I call resilience . . . the ability to come back from a disappointing performance or defeat with renewed dedication, enthusiasm and confidence. I've seen a lot of potentially great athletes side-tracked by defeat. But with Steve, it seems that with each defeat he becomes more steadfast in his determination. When someone beats him, rather than accept the fact that they might be better than he is, Steve sets his goal on turning around the result the next time they meet.

He had been defeated often enough by Coe, Cram and Ovett, so this was his moment.

America's other two runners were Jim Spivey from Eugene, twenty-four, a slim runner almost as light-weight as Coe, whose other option tended to be 5,000 metres, and Sydney Maree, twenty-seven, the black former South African champion who had gained US citizenship four months previously just in time for the US trials. With wretched luck, Maree was obliged to scratch the day before the first round because of an old injury. Robert Leach, the US Olympic committee's chief medical officer, announced that Maree could not compete without the chance of incurring a major injury to his knee, which he had partially torn after the trials. 'He has been under intensive treatment for the last six weeks but it has proven without success,' said Doctor Leach. Maree, who had gained the world record from Ovett in 1983, only to surrender it back to him almost immediately, was obliged to pull out of not just an Olympics but his long fight to escape from the apartheid-protesting sporting boycott of South Africa. By the next Olympics he would be thirty-one.

The ranking list as the runners went into the first round on 9 August was as follows:

3:34.20 – Hillardt (Australia); 3:34.50 – Ovett (GB); 3:34.51 – Gonzalez (Spain); 3:36.03 – Deleze (Switzerland); 3:36.22 – Thiebault (France); 3:36.43 – Spivey (USA); 3:36.48 – Cruz (Brazil); 3:36.63 – Wirz (Switzerland); 3:36.70 – Rogers

(New Zealand); 3:36.76 – Scott (USA); 3:37.03 – Morceli (Algeria); 3:37.08 – O'Donoghue (New Zealand); 3:37.00 – Cheruiyot (Kenya); 3:37.20 – Chesire (Kenya); 3:37.40 – O'Sullivan (Ireland); 3:39.70 – Coe (GB); 3:39.80 – Cram (GB)

There was nothing exceptional about Round One, except for the appearance of Ovett, and the sharp form again shown by Cruz. The British team management had spent some hours trying to get in touch with Ovett after his release from hospital the previous morning, because it seems they were not sure where he and his wife were staying. The LA organizing committee's chief medical officer for athletics, Dr Richard Greenspun, and Dr Steven Simons, pulmonary specialist at the LA orthopaedic hospital, had given a press conference at which they had outlined the recent history of Ovett's problems: bronchitis accompanied by wheezing at the time of the UK trials, then chest pains and breathlessness three weeks later; the development of numbness and tingling in the finger tips and hyperventilation during and on completion of four days of the 800; following which he had been given extensive heart and physiological tests.

Dr Simons had said that they had advised Ovett he could run if he wanted to; that he had no medical injury as such, but that they could not say what would be his level of performance in the 1,500, and that there could be a breakthrough of the symptons again at peak level. But here Ovett was. You have to admire the man's almost perverse courage, though Nick Whitehead and Lynn Davis, who had seen him in hospital on Tuesday evening, had considered he still looked unwell.

The first heat was notable for the fact that Rogers of New Zealand, who would go on to reach the final, only qualified in fourth place as one of the six fastest losers, behind Chesire, Khalifa and Mei of Italy; while Gonzalez of Spain, a potential medallist, was eliminated in fifth place.

Coe was in heat two, in which a group of seven ran together for much of the race up to 900 metres, in slowish time. Then Aden of Somalia, Coe, Donovan of Ireland and Thiebault of France moved away, Coe taking the lead 100 metres out, easing, and being passed by Thiebault at the line, just ahead of Vera of Spain, who would also go on to reach the final.

Ovett won the third heat in a singularly slow time and the pity here was that Deleze, a potential medallist, who was coming through for a comfortable qualifying place, caught one of Ovett's heels seven yards from the line, tripped, fell headlong and did not finish. Ovett revealed afterwards that his wife, Rachel, had not wanted him to race, and said that if he had thought he might have collapsed with a heart condition then obviously he would not have run. 'Today, I just wanted to run the first heat and see how it goes. I figured, what the hell, that's what I came here for. . . . I'm not trying to destroy myself, and if I'd felt anything serious, I would have stepped off the track. It was a matter of pride. I don't think I could have left the Olympics running as badly as I did in the 800 metres. I had to go back and run a bit better. I knew there was something seriously wrong [on Monday] when I hit the bell. It was as though someone had pulled out the power plug. I remember thinking "don't drop out". I was very unsteady and light-headed, and when the race finished I was thinking "don't faint on the track". When I got into the tunnel going out, it was very hot and claustrophobic, and that was the last I saw of the world until I woke up in hospital.'

Cruz and Scott dominated heat four, breaking away from the leading group after three laps, and Cruz covered the last 400 in 53.7. Hillardt qualified with a late run on the final straight; Zdravkovic, finalist in 1980, did not start, having been sent home by his Olympic committee for refusing to wear the contracted national shoe. The men with class, Abascal, Wirz and Becker, ran away from the pack on the last lap to take the places in heat five, while Cram and Spivey had the finishing speed to pull away over the final bend of heat six, hotly pursued by O'Donoghue in third place.

Coe, who hurried away for physiotherapy, admitted that he felt a bit worn down from the 800, and that for the first time the heat and smog were restricting his breathing, though not seriously. Scott's opinion was that Cruz would be favourite for the final if it was a slow race because of his finishing pace – though he didn't mention his private intention of ensuring it would *not* be slow. Cram simply said: 'With 200 metres to go in Saturday's final, I'll find out what shape I'm in.'

The surprise of the semi-finals was Cruz's failure to come to the line in the second heat. He had been scratched earlier in the day by Oliveira, for reasons which were a question of some dispute both inside and outside the Brazilian camp. Some Brazilian journalists were convinced that Oliveira, who is the stronger of the two personalities, was protecting a priceless reputation just achieved in the 800, with the excuse of a cold which might have helped Cruz to be beaten in either of the two remaining races. The Brazilian team doctor had seen Cruz and said that he was fit to run, but Oliveira denied this. 'Joaquim had understandably had no sleep on the night after the 800 because of his elation, and the following day he picked up the cold,' Oliveira explained to me later. 'We were definitely not pulling out to protect him, or to save him for Europe – that [his Permit appearances] was all agreed before LA. Joaquim had acupuncture on his feet to try to cure his cold, and to enable him to sleep, but it didn't help.'

The first semi-final was potentially the more severe, with ten of the twelve starters all serious candidates to reach the final and only the first four of each race and the next four fastest qualifying. Igohe of Tanzania led the first two laps, followed closely by Materazzi, Coe, Scott and Spivey. Down the second back straight Hillardt moved into fourth place and the order with two laps to go was Igohe, with a four-metre lead over Materazzi and Coe, another three metres separating a group of Hillardt, Scott and Abascal. Coming up to the bell, Abascal had closed to third, with Chesire moving in to fifth place. Round the penultimate bend Coe made his move, followed by Abascal and Scott, and now Rogers had also made contact. Down the back straight Abascal jumped two yards clear of Coe, Scott tried to go by, too, but Coe reacted instantly and held him off. Off the final bend Coe was going sweetly in second place with a group including Scott fighting it out just behind him. Over the last 50 metres Coe eased, carefully glancing each way over either shoulder behind him, as Scott moved through to take second place. Somehow, Coe failed to notice that both Chesire and Wirz were accelerating towards him as he slowed, about to pass him on each side. He made a lunge at the tape to beat them both by two-hundredths of a second. Yet had he been fifth instead of third – and another metre might have allowed them to get by before he could fully react – he could have been eliminated had his not been the faster heat. In the stands, Peter was shaking like a leaf as he helplessly watched this moment's aberration, and Seb would afterwards admit that he stood rigid with anxiety while he looked up at the huge television screen to watch the re-run, and see whether he had definitely made it in third place. In fact, the first seven from this heat went through. Chesire had moved from ninth at the bell to finish fourth, with a last lap of 54.7.

Against all exception, and some would say wisdom, the courageous Ovett now lined up with Cram and the rest in a bid to reach his third Olympic 1,500 final. It would not be as easy a race as he had had the previous day. Scammell of Australia and Khalifa led through the first lap, with Ovett third or fourth and Cram way back in eighth place behind Spivey. Scammell continued in front for another lap but down the third back straight he was passed by Khalifa and Mei, followed by Ovett and Spivey. By the bell Cram had voraciously closed to third and Scammell had fallen back to tenth. On the final bend, Cram kicked to take the lead and Ovett was still there three or four yards behind, giving it everything he had; coming into the home straight Ovett was second, but would drift to fourth at the line by two-hundredths of a second behind Spivey and Vera of Spain, while in the last 50 metres Mei dropped from fourth to seventh. Khalifa got the last of the twelve qualifying places just behind Ovett, who was again in distress at the finish and had to be helped to the medical centre. Predictably, he was weary and stressed and would be unable to say until the following morning if he could take up his place in the final.

1,500 metres Semi-final Splits

Heat 1 400			800		
	56.07	Igohe (Tanzania)		1:56.13	Igohe
	56.18	Materazzi (Italy)		1:56.25	Coe
	56.38	Coe (GB)		1:56.40	Materazzi
	56.52	Thiebault (France)		1:56.55	Hillardt

56.57	Abascal (Spain)	
56.68	Hillardt (Australia)	
56.69	Scott (USA)	
56.70	Bile (Somalia)	
56.83	Rogers (New Zealand)	
56.89	Wirz (Switzerland)	
56.90	Guimaraes (Brazil)	
57.13	Chesire (Kenya)	

1:56.55	Abascal
1:56.66	Scott
1:56.87	Wirz
1:56.87	Rogers
1:57.02	Bile
1:57.09	Thiebault
1:57.14	Guimaraes
1:57.33	Chesire

1,100

2:40.41	Coe
2:40.44	Abascal
2:40.63	Igohe
2:40.65	Scott
2:40.80	Materazzi
2:40.80	Rogers
2:40.94	Hillardt
2:40.96	Wirz
2:41.17	Chesire
2:41.32	Bile
2:42.16	Thiebault

1,200

2:54.72	Coe
2:54.77	Abascal
2:54.94	Scott
2:55.07	Materazzi
2:55.20	Rogers
2:55.26	Wirz
2:55.44	Chesire
2:55.46	Igohe
2:55.49	Bile
2:56.09	Hillardt
2:56.85	Thiebault

1,500

3:35.70	Abascal
3:35.71	Scott
3:35.81	Coe
3:35.83	Chesire
3:35.83	Wirz
3:36.48	Rogers
3:36.51	Materazzi
3:38.12	Hillardt
3:40.96	Thiebault
3:41.57	Igohe
d.n.f.	Guimaraes
disq.	Bile

Heat 2 **400**

55.95	Scammell (Australia)
56.18	Khalifa (Sudan)
56.39	Ovett (GB)
56.48	Mei (Italy)
56.50	Becker (West Germany)
56.63	Vera (Spain)
56.71	Spivey (USA)
56.77	Cram (GB)
56.94	O'Donoghue (New Zealand)
56.95	Jonga (Zimbabwe)
57.18	O'Sullivan (Ireland)

800

1:57.88	Scammell
1:57.92	Khalifa
1:57.96	Mei
1:58.10	Ovett
1:58.10	Spivey
1:58.12	Cram
1:58.17	Vera
1:58.26	Becker
1:58.38	O'Donoghue
1:58.38	O'Sullivan
1:58.69	Jonga

1,100	2:42.14	Mei		1,200	2:55.87	Mei
	2:42.25	Ovett			2:56.00	Ovett
	2:42.39	Cram			2:56.14	Cram
	2:42.43	Khalifa			2:56.28	Khalifa
	2:42.49	Spivey			2:56.33	Spivey
	2:42.66	Becker			2:56.53	Becker
	2:42.73	Vera			2:56.60	Vera
	2:42.96	O'Sullivan			2:57.17	O'Sullivan
	2:42.97	O'Donoghue			2:57.19	O'Donoghue
	2:43.32	Scammell			2:57.57	Scammell
	2:43.62	Jonga			2:57.95	Jonga

1,500	3:36.30	Cram
	3:36.53	Spivey
	3:36.53	Vera
	3:36.55	Ovett
	3:36.76	Khalifa
	3:37.28	Becker
	3:37.96	Mei
	3:38.71	O'Donoghue
	3:39.40	O'Sullivan
	3:40.83	Scammell
	3:41.80	Jonga

Seb had been spiked at some stage, not seriously, just under the knee, and there was some discussion about whether he should hurry back to the village or stay to watch the Decker–Budd bout with Peter and me. The cut already had a superficial dressing, so he opted for watching the women's 3,000-metre final. He was delighted with his own race, and gave a glowing feeling of well-being for all the scare he had given himself and his coach at the finish.

We watched Decker squander her platform as national heroine – which she had taken for granted before the race was run – by hustling Budd from behind with just over three laps to go, paying the ultimate penalty as she crashed off the track. Seb and Peter were instantly critical of Decker's tactics rather than Budd's. Victory became almost a formality for Maricica Puica of Rumania, with Wendy Sly of Britain taking the silver. Then we went back to my hotel, so that Peter and Seb could have a quiet tactical chat about the final. Yet in the time it took me to order tea from room-service, the chat was over. Peter: 'For Christ's sake, don't lose contact.' End of tactical talk. There was an air of tranquillity between them. Each of them knew, without the need to say anything, that Seb was in the best condition possible, relaxed and confident both mentally and physically. As we had left the stadium and Seb was chatting to a couple of friends, Peter had been bouncing up and down beside me like a ten-year-old. 'I really *do* believe it's going to happen,' he said, the care of all the years dropping away from him. I said we shouldn't tempt fortune by talking that way, though I was smiling: I believed it, too. After watching a re-run of the Decker disaster – Marty Liquori, ABC's commentator and a former 5,000 metres man, had the good grace to admit the next day he been wrong to blame Budd – we took Peter to catch his bus to Long Beach. Father and son embraced on the pavement, and said they'd see each other tomorrow after the race: two men at Camp Seven in sight of the summit.

I drove back slowly in the darkness to UCLA with Seb. He was in an unusual mood, calmer than I had ever seen him before, and I have been with him when he has fallen asleep in the passenger seat on the way to an AAA final. It was almost as if he was going off on holiday, rather than running in an Olympic final which was the climax of a year of super-human effort and determination to rescue a reputation, which *he* at least believed still had credibility. He and Peter were at ease. As he would say later, their agreed separation had given him all the input of Moscow, and none of the peripheral aggravation. 'Peter's major asset to me in coaching,' he said, 'has always been that while he's close, he's been incredibly analytical, especially in his construction of the training programme. I didn't want to dissipate this in LA. He was able to watch every race, in the stadium, without having to be with me and all the problems of co-ordinating our meeting points and travel. I could discuss with him on the phone next morning his analysis of how other runners had reacted, how their faces had looked at the finish, providing me with the information I couldn't get because I was not allowed to stay beside the track.' At Westwood, he jogged up the steps into the village, and I could tell that, remarkably, it was the run of a man who would sleep untroubled.

Like Ovett and Coe, Steve Cram also knew about Olympic
finals. He had been there as a nineteen-year-old, almost as an
observer, as it were, for the second duel between his compatriots
four years before. Maybe it was some of those recollections
which were getting through to him now. On the afternoon of the
final in LA, for which he was widely regarded as the favourite
even by Americans, he went to his room to try to get some rest,
but was down again after only a quarter of an hour, and spent
some while lazing in the sun, which is not the best preparation for
three and a half minutes of physical ordeal a few hours later. Were
nerves getting to the nerveless Geordie?

He had revealed, a few weeks before, in an exclusive interview
with David Barnes of the *Sunday People*, how his image of Ovett
as the supreme and confident champion, about to beat Coe, had
been altered by Ovett's behaviour prior to the 1,500 metres race
in Moscow:

> Suddenly all the doubts flooded in. He started talking to me about
> *if* he won the gold. He should have been saying *when*. But he was
> accepting the fact that he might get either silver or bronze. He was
> worried about Seb. He must have asked his coach, Harry Wilson,
> three or four times where Seb was, and whether he was warming up.
> Steve always had that special aura for me, and I had often wished I
> could be like him. But, for the first time, I was seeing him as a human
> being, just like the rest of us. So it was easier for me then to accept my
> own doubts before I went out to win the world championship in
> Helsinki . . . these things happen to everyone when they've got to
> go out and prove something in a single race . . . . [Before the
> Moscow race] I stepped into the lift with Ovett and Wilson on the
> way to the stadium for the final. It stopped a floor down, and Coe
> and his father Peter got in. There were just the five of us. It seemed an
> eternity until the lift reached the bottom floor. Someone mentioned
> the weather, but there was no escape from the awful atmosphere.
> Things were just as bad in the pre-race room, where all nine finalists
> were confined for fifteen minutes. I remember Seb pacing up and
> down the middle of the room in total silence. Then Steve got up to
> join him. They started chatting, but it was fairly inane stuff, like
> asking each other how they'd slept the night before. At least I'll
> know what to expect if, as I hope, the three of us are all penned up
> again in Los Angeles. . . .

Seb liked to keep away from other athletes. At the time we thought he was a snob, not wanting to stay with the rest of the team, but since I started winning medals, I've come to appreciate the need for avoiding all the hassle that comes your way. I now find Seb's attitude much more acceptable. . . . When I beat him in Gateshead just before going to Helsinki last year, it was a make-or-break race for him. I caught his eye just as I was completing a lap of honour. Seb grabbed me to shake hands and, knowing how he must have been feeling, that is a gesture I will never forget.

Was there now a reversal of roles? Winning and losing were perhaps on Cram's mind on that Saturday afternoon in LA. It may seem facile to say that Seb was thinking only of winning: if so, and from what he says, he was, then it could be at least part of the reason why he *did* win. His memories of the day are quite clear: 'I felt very good all day. With each race, including the 800s, I'd arrived at the stadium each time with more self-control. By the time I got to the final of the 1,500, I was a bit worried that if anything I was too relaxed. Some of the officials in the village, Nick and Lynn and Mary Peters [the women's team manager], who've seen a lot of me, were even concerned that I was so calm. This was one of the benefits of having sorted things out on my own. In LA, Peter and I had got back to sharing problems instead of doubling them. I remember your having mentioned Peter's comment in Moscow the night before the 1,500, that he'd 'give an arm and a leg' for me to win the next day. One doesn't need that. Now, I was coming out with fewer nerves and more concentration. From midday on that Saturday, I had no nerves, no thought of how I might be beaten. I was looking forward to it all the way through to the race. Moscow was do-or-die, but LA was clear cut. It was that concentration, that building up of aggression, which I found difficult not to show at the end. For six hours in LA, I wanted something more than I'd ever wanted anything. From the tunnel out on to the track, round the perimeter, there were no nerves. I wanted to be remembered as the athlete who came back.'

The medal ceremony for the 4x400 metres relay, in which Kriss Akabusi, Garry Cook, Todd Bennett and Phil Brown had taken the silver for Britain behind the USA, briefly delayed the start of the 1,500 final. The western end of the stadium was already in shadow as the twelve runners lined up as follows:

1   Joseph Chesire (Kenya)
2   Sebastian Coe (GB)
3   Steve Scott (USA)
4   José Abascal (Spain)
5   Andres Vera (Spain)
6   Steve Cram (GB)
7   Jim Spivey (USA)
8   Omar Khalifa (Sudan)
9   Peter Wirz (Switzerland)
10   Steve Ovett (GB)
11   Anthony Rogers (New Zealand)
12   Riccardo Materazzi (Italy)

The improvement of Khalifa over the past couple of years or so was about to be demonstrated. It was no brash moment, an extrovert seeking the limelight for a glorious half lap, which quickly took him to the front with Chesire, ahead of Materazzi and Coe. The smiling Sudanese is now an accomplished world class runner, and he was out there with real intent, leading after 400 with 58.9. The field was already quite spread, by almost a second, yet with Rogers by no means out of touch at the back together with Wirz. Ovett and Cram were seventh and eighth, trailing Abascal. Materazzi had stumbled, and almost fell at about 360 metres on the second bend.

Down the back straight for the second time Ovett lost ground and so, momentarily, did Scott before he accelerated past four men to go ahead of Coe (lying third), then jumped the front two to take the lead. It was the most unexpected of developments, but it was something Scott had planned a long while. As Len Miller, his coach, said later: 'For over a year we had thought about Steve making it a fast race. He's a great competitor, and he'd have been good enough to take the gold in Helsinki had he been level with Cram at 300, but Aouita got inside him and Steve had to run wide all round the last bend so that he probably covered three yards more than Cram and lost by less than that. So the intention in LA was to be sure that if no one else was pushing the race out after one lap, Steve would. He's run that way once or twice in the past and it's worked.'

Into the third bend, Khalifa and Chesire fractionally slowed from the surprise of Scott's burst, and Coe had to fend off Chesire with a touch on the shoulder. Off the bend and into the straight, Scott, with that erect stance, had opened a two-yard lead; Coe went past Khalifa, while another two yards or so farther back Cram had closed in, to form a line of three abreast with Chesire and Abascal, Spivey and Ovett being in close attendance behind them. Down the straight, Ovett made an unavailing effort to gain ground.

After 700 metes, with two laps to go, the order was: Scott, Coe, Khalifa and Abascal, Cram, Ovett, Chesire. Scott maintained his lead to the 800 mark in 1:56.8, a tenth of a second ahead of Coe, with Abascal a further two yards down. Into the fifth bend came Abascal, a shy and likeable man from Santander, who spends most of the year training in Catalonia as a member of Barcelona Football Club. He has no real finishing speed, and knew that he had to make his move from 600 metres out if he was to be in contention at the finish. He had never beaten his more applauded compatriot Gonzalez, but was now showing himself to be the one with resolution. He had been fifth in Helsinki.

If it had been Straub in Moscow whose courage had given the third and fourth laps of the final their scorching pace and had drained the kick out of Ovett, it was now Scott and then Abascal who on the second and third laps extended everyone but Coe. Coming into the straight towards the bell, Abascal and Coe had gone passed Scott, and Cram, Ovett and Spivey were following: Scott had shot his bolt. At the bell, Abascal (2:39) had two yards on Coe (2:39.3), who was a further two and a half yards ahead of Cram; Ovett was fourth and Scott was disappearing behind Spivey.

Sadly, Ovett's fortitude would end mid-way round the next bend. In his present condition, the pace was far beyond him and his chest pains were returning. Away went the rest towards the crescendo of the race, though now there were only three in the fight for the medals, as the dark haired Spaniard led Coe and Cram down the back straight. Ovett had run off the track.

Approaching the final bend, Cram gritted his teeth and drew alongside Coe and for a stride they were together shoulder to shoulder. But with a half-glance up into his rival's face as he came abreast, Coe kicked and went wide of Abascal, followed by Cram. On the crown of the bend, Coe gave a glance behind both ways, but there was only the one man with a chance of challenging him.

Entering the home straight, Coe had a lead of one and a half to two metres: and now he gave his third kick. It could not have hit Cram harder. As Coe accelerated away, poised and balanced and with his drive still as geometric as a steam engine's pistons, Cram's head was beginning to roll and his face twisted as he tried to respond. Way back, the rest of the field was streaming past the luckless Scott, with Chesire digging in for a vain bid for the bronze, followed by Spivey.

In the next forty metres, Coe had opened a full six metres on Cram, which he held to cross the line with an ecstatic smile and a new Olympic record of 3:32.53, lowering the sixteen-year-old Mexico City time, run by Keino, by over two seconds. Brave Abascal had the bronze as his reward behind Cram.

1,500 metres Final Splits

400	58.85	Khalifa (Sudan)	800	1:56.81	Scott
	58.88	Chesire (Kenya)		1:56.92	Coe
	58.94	Coe (GB)		1:57.10	Abascal
	59.08	Materazzi (Italy)		1:57.24	Khalifa
	59.10	Scott (USA)		1:57.31	Cram
	59.21	Cram (GB)		1:57.52	Ovett
	59.25	Abascal (Spain)		1:57.62	Chesire
	59.35	Ovett (GB)		1:57.73	Spivey
	59.36	Spivey (USA)		1:57.84	Rogers
	59.48	Vera (Spain)		1:57.90	Vera
	59.52	Wirz (Switzerland)		1:58.04	Wirz
	59.67	Rogers (New Zealand)		1:58.33	Materazzi
1,100	2:39.04	Abascal	1,200	2:53.21	Abascal
	2:39.28	Coe		2:53.21	Coe
	2:39.58	Cram		2:53.55	Cram
	2:39.75	Ovett		2:54.09	Chesire
	2:39.99	Scott		2:54.27	Spivey
	2:40.06	Spivey		2:54.51	Scott

	2:40.30	Chesire		2:54.74	Khalifa
	2:40.36	Khalifa		2:55.46	Vera
	2:40.92	Rogers		2:55.63	Rogers
	2:41.05	Wirz		2:55.80	Wirz
	2:41.09	Vera		2:56.86	Materazzi
	2:42.12	Materazzi			
1,500	3:32.53	Coe			
	3:33.40	Cram			
	3:34.30	Abascal			
	3:34.52	Chesire			
	3:36.07	Spivey			
	3:36.97	Wirz			
	3:37.02	Vera			
	3:37.11	Khalifa			
	3:38.98	Rogers			
	3:39.86	Scott			
	3:40.74	Materazzi			
	d.n.f.	Ovett			

Within seconds of victory, Seb's mood transformed from pleasure to a picture of almost anger. Turning towards the press and television ranks on his right, he looked up and with a scowl shouted out almost involuntarily: 'Who says I'm finished!' It was a long and lingering gesture. It was triumph over criticism as much as triumph over adversity. Yet was it also the inner reaction, bubbling once more to the surface, of the schoolboy of long ago who could not accept it when he was bowled out at cricket, who got nervous eczema in the tension of his eleven–plus examinations, who had now proved to the whole world that he was not the failure some had said him to be? The contemplation of success or failure can be equally motivating.

As Seb dissolved from his half-minute of specific aggression and ran off on his lap of honour, collecting a Union Jack on the way, his euphoria obscured from him the sight of Ovett still sitting on the ground, his arms and fingers bent in discomfort around his knees, his eyes glazed, while anxious medics wiped his brow and gently eased him on to a stretcher. With feeling, Seb said later: 'I was sorry for Steve, and sorry I didn't notice him there. It was brave of him to step out again after all he had been through in the 800.'

Abascal admitted that he had made his move too soon; that his coach had said he should wait until he was 500 out – in fact he had gone at 600. Whereas in Helsinki he had waited too long, today he had wanted to be nearer the front. 'I might have waited a little longer to kick if I'd realized the race was going so fast, but I was in a good position and felt comfortable. I got a little shakey with 300 metres to go, but I'm happy.'

Steve Scott was dejected but not broken. He had run to his plan but it had not worked. 'I wanted it to be a true miler's race, not a kicker's race. My thinking with Len Miller was that everyone would be dead on their feet at the end [if I made it fast from the second lap]. The opposite was true: *I* was dead on my feet! [He finished tenth.] I don't think the heat or air affected me at all. I'm used to it. It was cleaner than it has been. I was fairly calm before the race. The Olympics are pretty nerve-racking, and now I know why they only have them every four years. If they had them any more often, there would be a lot of athletic alcoholics. I just didn't have it today. I gave it all I had. It was a great experience. I had a great time.' Fine sentiments.

Len Miller was sorry for his athlete, worried in retrospect that he might not have given him the right advice. 'I have to admit that as we got close to the Games, it may have been my fault not to give Steve some warning, some guidance, because it became apparent that he was not as sharp as we would have liked. Possibly we should have run a time trial, but you tend not to want to do that, and to rely on the information from training. Anyway, Steve insisted right up to the night before that he was going ahead with the plan we had worked with for a year. In view of that, maybe I should have told him to ease it a little, not to go for the 2:39 at 1,100 which was his target [Scott went through in 2:40]. When I saw him in his room a while after the race he said he was OK. He has character, and he could take the disappointment. We've been eleven years together, our families and wives are close, we're more than just coach and athlete. He gave a smile and said "coach, maybe we still do something in '87 or '88". He's got courage.'

Before John Walker, competing in the 5,000, and Seb left the village for their respective finals, the 1,500 metre champion of 1976 had privately apologized to Seb for his statement sometime previously that no great athlete ever lasted at the top for more than two years. Cram, gold medallist of three championships during the two years of Seb's continual health problems, had said earlier in the fortnight that nobody would be able to last seven races over two distances in the abrasive acid and heat of Los Angeles's polluted air. Certainly Cruz had not.

If Cram was regretful at his failure to add the most prized title of all to his collection, it did not prevent him paying the most dignified of tributes to the winner. 'I'm satisfied. I enjoyed the race. I couldn't have done anything else. Seb was brilliant. I was beaten by a better athlete on the day. I didn't think Seb would have it in his legs. I didn't think *I* would. But he did and I'm pleased for him. I was surprised it went out so quick. Scotty moving on to the front as early as he did was such a surprise. He's not usually the type who goes out in front unless he's going for a world record. I thought if I got to the bell in 2:41, I'd be happy. In fact, Abascal was there in 2:39, which was two seconds faster. I think he wanted to run the kick out of Seb. Whether he did the right thing for himself, I don't know, but he gave it a go. My plan was to get to the front before the last 200, but I couldn't get there, it was so fast. It was a strong man's race and Seb was the man. Unless Seb's legs "went" down the [home] straight, I knew I had no chance. I was beaten by a brilliant athlete, one of the all time greats. My preparation has not been ideal. I've missed a lot of work, so to run 3:33 is encouraging. I think the world record is within my capabilities, but I'm not going to go round Europe chasing it.'

Ovett was at no conference. He had been taken to the medical centre, where he soon improved, and he had further extensive tests when he returned home. There had been a touch of the typical Ovett, who had sent a note to Zola Budd expressing sympathy for all the false accusations she had suffered for allegedly obstructing Decker. 'You weren't to blame for obstruction,' he said. 'I should know. After all, I invented it.'

The unsung heroes of Seb's victory were that bunch of anonymous Haringey club runners, John, Garry, Perry and Dennis, whose selfless running with Seb in the winter months had enabled him to recapture the endurance to withstand seven races. 'I think I showed that I was tougher, because I was getting better throughout the seven races,' Seb said. There was a timeless accolade in John Rodda's report in *The Guardian* two days later. Rodda, who has been on the international scene longer than any British correspondent, wrote:

The names ring out a resonant sound in any peel of Olympic bells – Paavo Nurmi, Jack Lovelock, Josef Barthel, Ron Delany, Herb Elliott, Peter Snell, Kip Keino and John Walker. The champions of the 1,500 metres have their own lofty place, but none so high as Sebastian Coe, the first man to win the title twice and with a style and power that would truly be acknowledged by all his forbears in the blue riband event of the Games. The celebration of the XXIII Olympiad in Los Angeles barely deserved such richness as the sight of Coe moving away from another Briton, Steve Cram, in the finishing stretch with a time of 3 minutes 32.53 seconds, an Olympic record surpassing Keino's at Mexico City in 1968. It was as near athletic perfection as possible on such an occasion, and for Coe probably the most satisfying race of a racing life littered with Himalayan peaks of drama. For over two years, Coe's career has been clogged by injury, illness and doubt, and it is a shivering thought that less than two months ago there was a considerable weight of opinion that Peter Elliott, not he, should get the third place in a British team. That British athletics was so close to tossing aside one of its greatest contributors to the Olympic Games and athletics is a matter for analysis on the return home.

The most revealing of Seb's recollections was that, after only a lap and a half, he was having to hold himself back. 'I felt good enough to have a go, to let rip there and then. I wondered before the race whether I could treat the first 700 as a warm up and then make it a race for all of the last two laps. The moment came and I had to decide. I'm glad now I didn't go, although I think I could have run under 3:30. The field was made up of "waiters". I'd thought that only Cram might wind it up from 600, but it was more likely he would wait to try and head me coming off the final bend. Scott's long run was a bit optimistic, but I had to cover his break. I didn't at that stage realize the pace was as fast as it was. A lap later, at 300 out, I remember turning and seeing a white vest, but no face, and wondering "which Steve?", because they're both taller than me. I looked again, and realized it was Cram.

'I kicked to go past Abascal, then again on the bend to hold off Cram. I was determined not to give Cram daylight, because he never wilts. Over the last 50 I seemed to be going quicker and quicker, not like the agony of Moscow. People talk about my kicks. The secret is that whenever you kick, it has to be effective in the first three or four strides: an instant effectiveness. There are two rules: never come upright, or let the line of your shoulders drop behind your hips, arching your back, and keep the drive forward. Secondly, *relax*, which is the hardest thing of all to do at speed.'

What was it that had precipitated that strange change of mood after the finish? He said he was surprised at his own feelings; the way his elation on crossing the line so suddenly changed back into aggression. Yet he thinks it was an extension of the aggression that had been there during the race. 'In Moscow, Straub was the only stimulus. Steve [Ovett] never came up on my shoulder, never came past. This time, three or four times I had to fight people. When they went by, I accelerated, so that having gone by they couldn't slow down. When Cram drew level on the final bend, I'd kicked twice already, so I had to be so much more clinically aggressive. Subconsciously, the comments of the past couple of years had probably been a motivation during the build-up, especially during the last few months as the Olympics approached. In a way, the comments were partly instrumental in the decision to go it alone after being beaten in the AAA championships [the *Mail's* headline was "Sebastian Slow"]. It was getting to the point where the outcome of my performances was not just landing at *my* feet. I felt I couldn't put Peter through that again. If I ran badly in the Games, I wanted to be the one to take the criticism, which I would in view of the argument over my selection for the 1,500. I've always been prepared to accept genuine criticism, especially if I made stupid errors. But in the past year some of the comments had transcended this.

'I was thrilled for Peter. As I walked out of the stadium with my mother, I said "I hope Peter is aware of what he's achieved".

At a time when most coaches would have clung, and been unnerved by the attitude of their athlete six weeks before the Games, Peter had the maturity to respond and be half of the initiative. Maybe that's the strength of a father-son relationship. The athletic challenge for both of us had been the seven races in nine days. It was, indeed, a dream come true.'

Nine

On to Stuttgart

Athletics is the show case of the Olympics. Of the three most illustrious figures of the Los Angeles Games, two were British. Carl Lewis emulated the four gold medals of Jesse Owens, Daley Thompson equalled Bob Mathias's two consecutive victories in the decathlon, and Sebastian Coe became the first modern Olympian to retain the metric mile title, as well as, disappointingly for him, the 800 metres silver medal. Not only because of these three exceptional athletes, it had been a memorable Games: unexpectedly friendly and hospitable in the land of the fast buck; predominantly efficient in its organization; and pleasingly relaxed and happy for the athletes in the villages. It had been a triumph for Peter Ueberroth and the organizing committee, in the face of five years of almost unbroken criticism, and it had been a generous gift to the sporting people of 140 nations from the 50,000 tirelessly courteous volunteers. More than five million spectators paid to see the Games live, ensuring a fat profit, with more than a million attending the football – thereby illuminating FIFA's error over the 1986 World Cup, which they had given to Mexico, and showing that what American soccer needs is not imported Beckenbauers, but ethnic identity. The traffic flowed and the air was reasonably clear, though some competitors suffered. There were neither terrorists nor the armed fanatics whom the Soviet bloc professed to fear. The Rumanians and Chinese came, finished second and fourth respectively in the medals table, and contributed greatly to the quality of performances. By the centenary Games of 1996, the Chinese could be challenging the Soviets, Americans and East Germans for supremacy.

The boycott did not work, again. Yet it was a pity that the Games of 1984 should have something of the reputation of the school playground swank and bully intimidating the rest of the kids: America drowned in an orgy of self-congratulation at the wholly deserved dominance of its competitors – though it must be said they are the products of an organized sporting system which others might do well to analyse rather than criticize. Joe Gergen of the *Los Angeles Times*, contemplating the continuing celebration of America's 174 medals with a five-day national tribute tour, reflected that it was 'another week to teach our children the wrong lesson not only about the nature of this event, but about the essence of sports'. Gergen goes on to relate the tale of a US hockey player, who became a part-time teacher in order to train with his Olympic squad, and was mocked by his pupils because he had no shiny limousine like the professional baseball and football stars. The pity of these Games was that through television they will only have served to make the average American, ignorant of almost anything outside his own country, more assertive.

It is too simple, however, to say that the now unreined gallop of commercialism, personified by Carl Lewis and his all too literal quest for gold, is the prime motivation of the competitors. True, we cannot stop the corruption of ideals and images which can follow the acquisition of Olympic fame. That has happened all down the century, and the evidence of it in Lewis's career is more the product of contemporary society than of the Olympics. What the International Olympic Committee must do, and is doing, is prevent corruption of the route to that Olympic fame. The Games *can* survive commercialism. The music of the jackpot comes to fewer than one per cent of the competitors: the majority know from the start they have not even a slim hope of becoming national, let alone international, affluent celebrities. Without such people as Elenora Mendonca of Brazil, who came forty-fourth and last in the women's marathon, the Games do not exist. Most fundamentaly, such are the standards of today's champions, that exceptional success can only come with the gift of rare ability nurtured by the years of anonymous preparation which must always precede fame. There are no short cuts to the victor's rostrum, even when the Soviet Union is absent. Lewis, Coe, Joan Benoit and Ed Moses had served their time. The 1984 Games had proved that sport among people who started by playing for fun, then moved onward in search of excellence, and only laterly became partially trapped by the jingoism of national pride, is still thriving. There had been no more memorable finish to any event than the cross-country climax of the modern pentathlon, some of whose competitors, such as Richard Phelps from Gloucestershire, subsidized their own training expenses.

The Olympics is still about real life, its fears and joys, whatever the hype and banality some commentators may give it. There is not one person in a thousand among those who beg Seb Coe for his autograph who could tolerate for one month the schedule of discipline, and often pain, with which he has lived for more than fourteen years. In their concern for the Games it is not necessary for the IOC to exclude the professionals, whose advance in some sports is inexorable, and of itself not reprehensible, in an era where excellence must necessarily equate with time spent achieving it. Instead, the IOC should halt medical cheating with drugs, and the appropriation by independent commercial sports organizers of large numbers of competitors, thereby side-tracking huge areas of revenue away from the federations, whose largely voluntary work is the pyramid base of all sports.

The IOC can, with vigilance, eliminate the use of drugs. Tests on two weight-lifters, who finished fourth and ninth, were found to be positive and they were subsequently banned for life by their own international federation. This attitude should be mandatory throughout the Games, as should random testing outside the four-yearly event. The ascent of potential professionals will inevitably increase drug abuse. I would like to think the IAAF would ban the Finnish runner, Vainio, for life when his drug's test was positive after he won the 5,000 silver medal – which he subsequently refused to return. The IAAF have maintained ambivalent attitudes on reinstatement, though John Holt, the general secretary, is anxious that they should become less equivocal.

The expediency which cannot be eliminated is the deliberate

manipulation of performance by outstanding athletes for their own convenience, a debate generated in Los Angeles by Lewis and Thompson. Lewis deliberately declined to attempt the world record in the long jump, because he no doubt considered that there might be greater benefit from such an achievement on another occasion (though, to be fair, he was running the 200 metres heats on the same day and he said that his thigh was stiffening). Thompson, however, quite clearly stepped back from a possible world record when he ran his final decathlon event, the 1,500 metres, in a time substantially outside his personal best, missing the record by only a fraction. There can be no legislation against this, only regret from the paying customer.

It would be naive to pretend that these days Seb does not profit substantially from his sport. He is open about it. What he and Peter are both sensitive to is retaining the true quality of the sport which provides the money. As far as I am aware, Seb has never run a single race since he became a senior international in which he was not either trying to win, to break a record, or to explore his own potential with some piece of front running. In other words, he has never short-changed the paying public by not giving his best on the day. The same cannot be said of many of the athletes who go touring the circus of Permit Meetings at the end of each season. We know very well that some athletes are not running to win, but are only there to make up the numbers, and for the appearance money they can now legitimately negotiate. It is this attitude which was the subject of widespread criticism from Pat Butcher in *The Times*, Christopher Brasher in the *Observer* and Cliff Temple in *The Sunday Times* immediately following the Olympic Games in Los Angeles. It was provoked by the fact that in Zurich, where Seb has twice broken world records in a series of outstanding attempts over six years, Aouita and Seb were kept apart in separate attacks on the mile and 1,500-metre records, when the public and press would have liked to see them racing each other.

They were kept apart not by their own wishes, but the decision of the promoter, Andreas Brugger, who believed that had they been in the same race it would have been slow and tactical, rather than a record attempt. The controversy was fuelled by the fact that Aouita was said to have stated after the Olympics that Seb only won the 1,500 because he, Aouita, had been running in the 5,000, which he duly won, and that he could not wait for the chance to beat Coe and to overhaul Ovett's world record. Yet Aouita himself told Brugger that he would race only to beat Seb, and not to break the record, which persuaded Brugger to put him in a separate event. Seb would also have been happy to compete against Aouita in a field which already included eight other Olympic 1,500 competitors, and particularly because he himself was in the best condition he had been in for three years. The probability is that he will be running few serious 1,500s from next season onwards, when he will be concentrating on the 5,000 metres. In the event, both runners failed to break the records in their races, though Seb won an outstanding race, inside his Olympic record and with his third fastest time. It has to be said in Brugger's defence that record-breaking is what has generated wide public and television interest over recent years at meetings in Zurich, Brussels, Oslo, Cologne, Koblenz, Rome and elsewhere. However, this attitude becomes tatty when the attempts too consistently fail, which inevitably they must. That is not necessarily the fault of the athletes. Of course they cannot race three times a week and produce their best, and Seb has never been a party to allowing this to happen. The pattern of his racing programme shows that, over the years, he has consistently competed in many fewer races than most competitors, with a higher average standard as his twelve world records demonstrate.

The argument is that top athletes deliberately avoid each other, pick their races in order to remain unbeaten, thus protecting their prestige and ensuring a higher bargaining price for their appearance. What Peter Coe has persistently maintained is that the larger sums of money are to be had from commercial endorsements off the track, and that the athlete aiming for excellence in the major championships should tailor his racing programme exclusively to that end. As he said, and I have mentioned it before: 'Seb has never run a race, anywhere at any time, which was not a part of his carefully scheduled programme of training and racing designed to produce a few peaks in championships or the occasional world record attempt.'

It is no use pointing out, as critics of the record–chasing circus do, that the top players in tennis and golf, and in team games such as soccer, meet each other regularly. In team games they are committed to do so by the fixture list, and to an extent the same is true in, say, tennis, where McEnroe and Lendl are capable of playing a dozen major tournaments a year and countless lesser ones without a visible deterioration in their performance which is easily detectable by the public. This is not so in an exactly measured sport such as athletics. Therefore it is reasonable and understandable that the top performers in athletics should not wish to expose themselves more than two or three times each year to their most accomplished rivals, when the stakes are so high, on any occasions other than when they can plan and expect to be at a peak. They are, to some extent, moving towards the same arena as prize fighters who usually want a return clause written into the contract for a title bout.

The situation in the Permit Meetings is likely to be altered by the institution, from 1985, of a Grand Prix under the control of the IAAF, by which athletes will, for the first time, be entitled to compete in a series of meetings for points. The prize money will be paid per meeting, and also on an aggregate basis, and will be paid into their trust funds. This will oblige athletes to race tactically rather than for records, and will restore a sense of regular competition, especially as there will be double the points for participation in the concluding meeting of the season.

The outcome of this must inevitably be to raise the levels of what is professionalism by any other name. The IAAF will need to guard against the danger that the Grand Prix will become a stronger attraction for the athletes than the major championships: Commonwealth, African, Asian, Pan-American, European, World and Olympic. It may become necessary, therefore, eventually to embrace the various championships as part of the Grand Prix, as in tennis, to ensure participation. An insuperable aspect of all athletics competition with a commercial element is that sprinters and field events competitors are capable of competing more often, close to a reasonable peak, than are the middle-distance runners who are the focal point of public interest.

Seb flew home from LA and, before going on to his first Permit Meeting appointment in Zurich, stopped off to run a gentle 1,500 for Haringey, helping them to a one-and-a-half point victory over Wolverhampton for their first Guardian Royal Exchange League title, and the right to stage next year's European Clubs Final. There was disappointment that he had not run in the Nike meeting at Crystal Palace the night before, but he regarded the club fixture as a priority. It was, in part, repayment for his mistake earlier in the season of arranging a Loughborough event on the same weekend as a League fixture. As he said to Neil Allen in the *Standard*:

> I sympathize with the pull on athletes because these Permit Meetings, let's be straight about it, pay the mortgage. But the powers-that-be must make sure that the interests of the clubs is never overlooked. Their needs and their fixtures should get full recognition. To give just one example, we have a coach at Haringey, John Isaacs, who trained six athletes to Olympic selection, three of them becoming finalists. Yet he was not officially accredited for the Games. That can't be right. My father, who coaches just one athlete, *was* accredited.

Seb was sceptical about reports that Ed Moses was to get $100,000 if he beat his own world record in Zurich. In fact, Moses asked for $25,000, a request which was rejected by Brugger, and he did not run. 'In my case I've no doubt there will be pacemakers laid on for me. Brugger is not going to miss the chance of a middle-distance record. To be honest, if it's there, if the pace is just right, I'll give it all I've got. But it's not quite like some other seasons, when world records have seemed pretty important. I feel so fulfilled by all that's happened at the Olympics.'

Seb was unsure about the comments attributed to Aouita and his belief that he could have beaten Coe in the Olympic 1,500. 'That guy went for the easier of two events, the one where he thought he was more sure of a medal. In the Olympics, which only come every four years, you don't turn your back on what seems allegedly the easier race. I think Aouita's attitude was similar to John Walker's, who didn't think he could match the

1,500 field, whatever way the race was run. John made a careful decision and I'm sure that's what Aouita will have done. The 5,000 did not have the same depth, even if the final was one of the fastest times ever. Plenty of the people in distance running in Britain would do the first round of the 5,000 run in LA – about fourteen minutes – regularly in training. A semi-final in 13:28 was an easier option than a 1,500 semi-final in 3:35. I don't want to run Aouita down, he's capable of breaking both records. But you cannot say someone else won a race because you weren't there, when you've deliberately avoided it, knowing some of the opposition will already have had four previous races.'

In Zurich, the mile was scheduled before the 1,500. Stanley Redwine of America set a near perfect pace for two laps, passing the half-mile in about 1.54. Hillardt of Australia then took over, followed by Aouita and Walker, ahead of a pack including the Americans Chuck Aragon and Todd Harbour, and Irishman Ray Flynn. At the bell, in around 2:54, Aouita had left himself too much to do; besides which he was showing an evident disinterest, and only really started to exert himself over the last 300. His time of 3:49.54 was two seconds outside Seb's three-year-old record, but in second place Walker, that most evergreen of great runners, produced 3:50.27, a pace which might have given him a medal in the Olympic 1,500.

Out of a shambles of bad planning by the organizers, Seb produced an expert performance to win the 1,500. The frustration was that a chance had been squandered, one of the best he had ever had, of recapturing the record on a night when he was at an absolute peak. Once before, for three quarters of an hour in Oslo in 1980, he had held the four records simultaneously, from 800 through 1,000 and 1,500, up to the mile. Immediately he had claimed the 1,000, on to the track came Ovett to steal the mile record, only a week before their dramatic head-to-head in Moscow.

Some strained fibres in Seb's foot, which required some careful strapping, were no impediment in Zurich but, further strained by the race, would make it his last of the year, obliging him to withdraw from subsequent appearances planned for

Cologne, Rome, and Crystal Palace. The shambles lay in the pacing: perhaps part of the problem was that Brugger was unwell, but when record attempts, especially by the most prolific record breaker in history, are the very essence of Brugger's co-ordination of the biggest and best of the Permit Meetings, to make a mess of the planning was to serve champange in cardboard cups. The man selected to run the first two laps was the American, James Robinson, whose speciality is the half mile. Yet, as Peter said at the time, the only ideal pace-maker is a runner with the capacity still to be in contention himself at the end of the race or, if anything, a runner with a capacity for longer rather than shorter races, like Chataway with Bannister thirty years before. It would be unfair to blame Robinson, but on this occasion he went off far too slowly, and was boxed in the middle of the pack after 50 metres, with Seb leading the field and having to wait until the first home straight for Robinson to extricate himself and at last get to the front. The other mistakes by the organizers were in having a field of fifteen, which is far too crowded for a record attempt, and in not placing Coe and Robinson together on the outside of the start-line, from where they could make an uncluttered run for the first bend, but towards the inside – and not even together. By the time Robinson reached the 800 in 1:55.7, the chance of the record was already past. Furthermore, at such a comparatively undemanding pace, Seb suddenly found himself not so much in a record attempt as under some pressure to hold off and beat the efforts of Scott, Deleze, Abascal, Spivey, Materazzi, Nemeth of Austria, Wirz and Busse (East Germany). It was certainly still a race to provide entertainment for a full house. At the bell, 2:39.3, Seb led Abascal and Busse, but any one of six was poised to challenge him. As in the Coliseum twelve days before, he put in his kick on the final bend and shot away from everyone to win in 3:32.39. For Scott, there was the consolation after his Olympic failure to come with a beautifully judged late run for second place.

Apart from Evelyn Ashford, silencing those critics who had claimed the Olympics were counterfeit because of the absence of the Soviet block when she convincingly beat Marlies Gohr of East Germany in the 100 metres with the only world record of the evening in 10.76, the other excitement of the meeting came from Cruz. Recovered from his cold and the mental exhaustion of LA, he ran a personal best in his attack on Seb's 800 record, with 1:42.34: a time surpassed only by Seb's world records of 1979 (1:42.33) and 1981 (1:41.72). Cruz demonstrated his phenomenal strength over a period of two weeks with the best sequence of runs ever put together, the peak of which was his 1:41.77, four days after Zurich in Cologne and five-hundredths of a second outside Seb's record. Cruz now has three of the five fastest 800s ever run, though in Nice a week earlier he had found the 1,000 metres a shade too far in his attack on that distance, and one wonders whether his limit at 1,500 may be less than we imagine. We should discover next season, when he must surely erase Seb's 800 metre record, which has been regarded, together with Beamon's long jump, as the world record of world records.

The irony for Seb in Zurich was that an hour or so after his run he met Omar Khalifa in the lift back at the hotel. 'You should have asked me,' said Khalifa with that friendly grin. 'I'd have given you the right time at 800.' Seb also had reason to envy Steve Cram two days later in Brussels, where Cram received the perfect pacing but found there was not enough in his legs to get him near to Ovett's record. The 3:30 barrier remains intact for another year, yet Seb is convinced it was within his grasp that week. It was galling to recall that three years earlier in Stockholm, on a perfect night when he had also been at a peak, Seb had suffered another of Robinson's misjudgements. On that occasion, Robinson had gone off far too fast, had got out of touch, and Seb had been left in isolation for the entire three-and-three-quarter laps, running 3:31.95, which remained his personal best.

After the Olympics, Cram had reflected that it might be the end of an era for him and Seb; that possibly they would never run seriously against each other again if Seb was moving up to 5,000 in future. 'It saddens me,' admitted Cram, 'that I never beat him over the mile or 1,500 metres.' It seems that Cram's intention is to remain running over four laps. By the 1988 Olympics he will be twenty-seven, the same as Seb was in Los Angeles. Will Cram still have the emminence at that distance by then as he does now, or might he be advised, like Coe, to try moving up to twelve and a half laps, with plenty of time to accommodate to the different demands? Dave Moorcroft, seventh in the 1,500 metres at the 1976 Olympics, stepped up a distance to avoid the Coe-Ovett dominance which developed at 1,500. Moorcroft failed to produce his best in Moscow and Los Angeles, in spite of his world record at 5,000 in 1982. Talking of the switch in distances, he said: 'A lot of 1,500 metres men think they can juggle with my distance and be an instant success. I read every week of athletes being advised to step up, as if it was the simple formula for success. What nonsense. Very few can do it. Look at history: the only ones to succeed in modern times are Eamonn Coghlan, Brendan Foster and Thomas Wessinghage.' Modestly, Moorcroft excluded his own world record coupled with the Commonwealth title in 1982. How would Seb find the switch?

'Winning in LA has restored my confidence,' he says. 'It's left me in a nice position to be able to concentrate on another distance. I know that at thirty-two, in Seoul, I can't except to put two 800s back to back, never mind four. I might just be in with a shout at 800 in the European Championships in Stuttgart in 1986. Yet I can leave the 800 now, with a tinge of disappointment, even without a major title to show for my dominance of the distance. I can take nothing away from Cruz's achievement this year. At 1,500 I don't need to prove anything. I'm free, I've no dues to pay. Going on for the 5,000 is as serious a part of my career as anything in the past. I wouldn't otherwise waste two years, and I'll want to be going for a medal in Stuttgart. I agree totally with Dave Moorcroft, it's not an easy or simple job moving up. It took him two years to adjust, and I would be unwise to think it would take me any less. It's mental as well as physical. I've been used to either one and half minutes on the track or nearly four. Now it's going to be thirteen, and I need to remember than 5,000 metre men are now running 1:56 for the last 800. It's a challenge.

'One thing I'm particularly pleased about is that I have proved you don't need drugs to win Olympic titles at middle-distance running. [One British national newspaper correspondent was openly claiming in Los Angeles that Coe's performance over recent years showed he *had* to be on drugs.] Firstly, just look at me, at my frame. Anyone accusing me of this is saying that what I'm doing is not just a combination of talent and hard work. From November of 1983 to April this year, I was doing ten hours a week in the gym, working harder than I've ever worked before: so hard, I had to have four pairs of trousers let out because of the build-up of thigh mucle. I don't know enough about drugs even to recognize the signs which might show that I was using them, but as a member of the IOC Athletes Commission, I firmly believe that anyone found positive should be banned for life. How many times do the sceptics want me to be tested? It's already about fourteen times, including a domestic championships. Any administrative body can come and give me a random test any time they like. It's odd that Vainio from Finland should be found positive: from the country where one of their newspapers accused me of drug-taking and not being able to turn up in Helsinki. They should clean up their own house first. It's sad that Finland, a country which has been such a pioneer in running, should have fallen foul of the rules.'

Seb, arguably the greatest middle-distance runner of his age, has mixed feelings about the commercial turmoil in which he finds himself. 'I'm glad I still have the independence to do what I want. What will the pressures be in ten years time! I'd rather have my time now. [In spite of the money] I've never thought of my athletics as a career. Ovett and I took up the sport because we enjoyed it. Had I been commercially minded, I'd have been better not to risk this season [in competition]. I could have ended up with nothing. Who in their right mind would have taken the risk in the light of the past two years? I could have surrendered everything in the way of potential sponsorship. The area we're into is a cold equation of reality. Ovett and I not only pioneered the new age, we've been dragged into it. There's an element of responsibility to try to protect the ethics of the sport, just as there should have been when Jimmy Hill got rid of the maximum wage in soccer.'

He hopes that he will be able to rediscover a friendly working relationship with all the press after a year of tension and relative withdrawal of communication with all but two or three journalists. 'I was grateful, for example, that David Emergy should so generously withdraw some of his earlier criticism when I won in LA. I wouldn't want their life or mine to be any harder than it already is. Over the next two years I'd want to be able to talk to them like the old days. I've made my point on the track, which is what I cared about.' Seb is optimistic that there will still be sufficient in his legs between now and 1986 for it to be worthwhile, on both sides, for him to go back to the press box. If, over the next two summers, he finds he is running sweetly at 5,000 metres, he might even be there waving at the media in the 1987 World Championships or the 1988 Olympics. No one since Nurmi has ever triumphed over such a wide range at the Olympics. That *would* be something at which to aim!

Appendix A

A complete list of the track races in which Sebastian Coe has competed

Abbreviations

pb-personal best   sf-semi final   UK-United Kingdom record
h-heat   cr-championship record   WR-World record
f-final   CR-Commonwealth record   OR-Olympic record
★-on cinders

Date	Event	Track	Distance	Place	Time
1973 (aged 16)					
17 March	UK Indoor Championships	Cosford	800 m	4th	2:2.5
1 May	B. Milers' Club	Stretford	800 m	3rd	1:56.6
5 May	Longwood Youth	Huddersfield	1,500 m	1st	4:7.4
13 May	B. Milers' Club	Crystal Palace	800 m	2nd	1:56.0(pb)
18 May	West District Schools	Sheffield	800 m	1st	2:1.1
18 May	West District Schools	Sheffield	1,500 m	1st	4:15.4
23 May	Sheffield Selection	Sheffield	3,000 m	1st	8:43.7
3 June	Northern League	Sheffield	1,500 m	3rd	4:7.5
9 June	Yorks Schools Championships	York	3,000 m	1st	8:49.0
16 June	N. Counties	Sheffield	1,500 m	3rd	3:59.5(pb)
7 July	English Schools	Bebington	3,000 m	1st	8:40.2(pb)
17 July	S. Yorks League	Doncaster	800 m	1st	1:59.7
21 July	City Championships	Sheffield	800 m	1st	1:57.0
21 July	City Championships	Sheffield	1,500 m	1st	4:7.4
4 Aug	AAA Youth Championships	Aldersley	1,500 m	1st	3:55.0(pb)
14 Aug	Stretford League	Manchester	3,000 m	6th	8:34.6(pb)
9 Sept	Hallam Harriers Championships	Sheffield	400 m		51.8(pb)
15 Sept	Rotherham Festival	Rotherham	1,500 m	1st	3:58.0
1974 (aged 17)					
10 April	Training run	Rotherham	800 m		1:55.1 (pb)
April-Nov	Injured with stress fractures				
1975 (aged 18)					
21 March	Indoor Under 20 Championships	Cosford	1,500 m(h)	2nd	4:8.0
22 March	Indoor Under 20 Championships	Cosford	1,500 m(f)	1st	3:54.4(pb)
13 April	Pye Cup	Cleckheaton	1,500 m	1st	3:49.7(pb)
30 April	B. Milers' Club	Rawtenstall	1,500 m	1st	3:54.0
31 May	Yorks Senior Championships	Cleckheaton	1,500 m	1st	3:51.3
8 June	Pye Cup	Cleckheaton	800 m	1st	1:53.8(pb)
8 June	Pye Cup	Cleckheaton	4 x 400 m		50.5
21 June	N. Counties Under 20	Gateshead	1,500 m	1st	3:50.8
25 June	Northern League	Sheffield	300 m	2nd	36.2(pb)
28 June	N. Counties Under 20	Blackburn	3,000 m	1st	8:14.2(pb)
26 July	AAA Junior Championships	Kirkby	1,500 m(h)	1st	3:52.0

27 July	AAA Junior Championships	Kirkby	1,500 m(f)	1st	3:49.1(pb)
30 July	GB v France/Spain	Warley	1,500 m	1st	3:50.3
23 Aug	European Junior Championships	Athens	1,500 m(h)		3.48.0(pb)
24 Aug	European Junior Championships	Athens	1,500 m(f)	3rd	3:45.2(pb)

1976 (aged 19)

24 Jan	UK Indoor Championships	Cosford	1,500 m	5th	3:51.0
6 March	Loughborough Match	Crystal Palace	4 x 800 m		1:52.0(pb)
20 March	Loughborough Match	Cosford	600 relay/leg		80.4(pb)
28 March	B. Milers' Club	Stretford	1,500 m	1st	3:47.4
14 April	H. Wilson Mile	Crystal Palace	1 mile	1st	4:7.6
1 May	B. Milers' Club	Stretford	1 mile	1st	4:5.7(pb)
12 May	Loughborough Match	Loughborough	800 m	1st	1:53.0
16 May	Yorkshire Championships	Cleckheaton	1,500 m	1st	3:43.3(pb)
19 May	Loughborough v Borough Rd	Isleworth	800 m	1st	1:53.0
31 May	Inter–Counties Championships	Crystal Palace	1 mile	2nd	4:2.4(pb)
11 June	Olympic Selection	Crystal Palace	1,500 m	7th	3:43.2(pb)
17 June	Loughborough v AAA	Loughborough	800 m	1st	1:50.7(pb)
24 July	Heckington Sports	Heckington	1 mile	1st	4:9.1
1 Aug	Open Meeting	Nottingham	1,000 m	1st	2:30.0
8 Aug	B. Milers' Club	Stretford	800 m	1st	1:47.7(pb)
13 Aug	AAA Championships	Crystal Palace	1,500 m (h)	3rd	3:45.05
14 Aug	AAA Championships	Crystal Palace	1,500 m (f)	4th	3.42.6(pb)
21 Aug	Rediffusion Games	Gateshead	1 mile	3rd	4:1.7(pb)
30 Aug	Emsley Carr Mile	Crystal Palace	1 mile	7th	3:58.3(pb)
14 Sept	Bell's Games	Gateshead	1 mile	2nd	4:0.5

1977 (aged 20)

29 Jan	UK Indoor Championships	Cosford	800 m	1st	1:49.1(pb/CR)
19 Feb	GB v W. Germany	Dortmund	800 m	1st	1:47.6(CR)
26 Feb	GB v France	Cosford	800 m	1st	1:47.5(CR)
12 March	European Indoor Ch'ships	San Sebastian	800 m(h)	1st	1:50.5
13 March	European Indoor Ch'ships	San Sebastian	800 m(sf)	1st	1:48.25
14 March	European Indoor Ch'ships	San Sebastian	800 m(f)	1st	1:46.54(CR)
3 July	Dewhurst Games	Spalding	800 m	1st	1:51.7
23 July	AAA Championships	Crystal Palace	800 m	2nd	1:46.8(pb)
30 July	Philips Games	Gateshead	800 m	2nd	1:47.4
14 Aug	Europa Cup	Helsinki	800 m	4th	1:47.6
16 Aug	Ivo Van Damme	Brussels	800 m	3rd	1:46.3(pb)
24 Aug	Club Meeting	Rotherham	400 m	1st	49.1
28 Aug	GB v W. Germany	Crystal Palace	800 m	1st	1:47.8
29 Aug	Emsley Carr Mile	Crystal Palace	1 mile	1st	3:57.7(pb)
7 Sept	Courage Games	St Ives	800 m	1st	1:48.1
9 Sept	Coca-Cola	Crystal Palace	800 m	2nd	1:44.95(UK)

1978 (aged 21)

26 April	Loughborough Match	Loughborough	400 m	1st	48.0(pb)
10 May	Loughborough Match	Isleworth	400 m	1st	47.7(pb)
14 May	Yorkshire Championships	Cleckheaton	800 m	1st	1:45.6(CR)
1 June	Loughborough v AAA	Loughborough	800 m	1st	1:50.0
9 July	Philips Games	Gateshead	800 m	1st	1:46.8
15 July	UK Championships	Meadowbank	800 m	1st	1:47.1
9 Aug	International Invitation	Viareggio	800 m	1st	1:45.7
18 Aug	Ivo Van Damme	Brussels	800 m	1st	1:44.26(UK)
31 Aug	European Championships	Prague	800 m	3rd	1:44.8
15 Sept	Coca-Cola	Crystal Palace	800 m	1st	1:43.97(UK)
17 Sept	McEwans Games	Gateshead	1 mile	1st	4:2.2

1979 (aged 22)

27 Jan	UK Indoor Championships	Cosford	3,000 m	1st	7:59.8

25 April	Loughborough Match	Crystal Palace	400 m	2nd	48.3
20 May	Yorkshire Championships	Cleckheaton	800 m	1st	1:50.5
21 May	Yorkshire Championships	Cleckheaton	400 m	1st	47.6(pb)
23 May	Loughborough Match	Loughborough	400 m	1st	47.4(pb)
23 May	Loughborough Match	Loughborough	800 m	1st	1:54.8
31 May	Loughborough v AAA	Loughborough	800 m	1st	1:47.8
16 June	N. Counties Championships	Costeloe Park	800 m	1st	1:46.3
30 June	Europa Cup	Malmo	800 m(sf)	1st	1:46.63
3 July	Bislet Games	Oslo	800 m	1st	1:42.33(WR)
14 July	AAA Championships	Crystal Palace	400 m	2nd	46.85(pb)
17 July	Golden Mile	Oslo	1 mile	1st	3:48.95(WR)
5 Aug	International Invitation	Viareggio	800 m	1st	1:50.0
8 Aug	Europa Cup	Turin	800 m(f)	1st	1:47.3
15 Aug	Weltklasse	Zürich	1,500 m	1st	3:32.03(WR)

1980 (aged 23)

26 April	Loughborough Match	Crystal Palace.	3,000 m	1st	7:57.4
7 May	Loughborough Match	Isleworth	1,500 m	1st	3:45.1
11 May	Yorkshire Championships	Cudworth	5,000 m	1st	14:6.0
21 May	England v Belgium	Crystal Palace	800 m	1st	1:47.5
25 May	Inter-Counties Championships	Birmingham	800 m(h)	1st	1:49.0
26 May	Inter-Counties Championships	Birmingham	800 m(f)	1st	1:45.41
1 June	International Invitation	Turin	800 m	1st	1:45.8
5 June	Loughborough v AAA	Loughborough	800 m	1st	1:44.98(WR)★
7 June	N. Counties	Cleckheaton	800 m	1st	1:44.7
14 June	UK Championships	Crystal Palace	400 m	2nd	47.0
1 July	Bislet Games	Oslo	1,000 m	1st	2:13.4(WR)
24 July	Olympic Games	Moscow	800 m(h)	1st	1:48.5
25 July	Olympic Games	Moscow	800 m(sf)	1st	1:46.7
26 July	Olympic Games	Moscow	800 m(f)	2nd	1:45.9
30 July	Olympic Games	Moscow	1,500 m(h)	2nd	3:40.1
31 July	Olympic Games	Moscow	1,500 m(sf)	1st	3:39.4
1 Aug	Olympic Games	Moscow	1,500 m(f)	1st	3:38.4
8 Aug	Coca–Cola	Crystal Palace	800 m	1st	1:45.0
13 Aug	Weltklasse	Zürich	1,500 m	1st	3:32.19
14 Aug	International Invitation	Viareggio	800 m	2nd	1:45.01

1981 (aged 24)

24 Jan	AAA Indoor Championships	Cosford	3,000 m	1st	7:55.2
11 Feb	GB v GDR (Indoor)	Cosford	800 m	1st	1:46.0(WR)
3 May	UAU Championships	Crystal Palace	400 m	1st	46.9
13 May	Loughborough Match	Borough Road	400 m	1st	47.4
17 May	Yorkshire Championships	Cleckheaton	800 m	1st	1:46.3
3 June	England v USA/Eth/Bel	Crystal Palace	800 m	1st	1:44.06
3 June	England v USA/Eth/Bel	Crystal Palace	4 x 400		45.7
7 June	GB v USSR	Gateshead	4 x 400		46.5
10 June	International Invitation	Florence	800 m	1st	1:41.72(WR)
5 July	Europa Cup	Helsinki	800 m	1st	1:47.57
7 July	International Invitation	Stockholm	1,500 m	1st	3:31.95(pb)
11 July	Bislet Games	Oslo	1,000 m	1st	2:12.18(WR)
17 July	GB v USSR	Gateshead	800 m	1st	1:47.4
19 July	Dairygate	Leicester	1,000 m	1st	2:17.4
31 July	Talbot Games	Crystal Palace	800 m	1st	1:46.67
5 Aug	International Invitation	Viareggio	800 m	1st	1:47.12
7 Aug	AAA Championships	Crystal Palace	800 m(sf)	1st	1:45.89
8 Aug	AAA Championships	Crystal Palace	800 m(f)	1st	1:45.45
15 Aug	Europa Cup	Zagreb	800 m	1st	1:47.03
19 Aug	International Invitation	Zürich	1 mile	1st	3:48.53(WR)
28 Aug	Golden Mile	Brussels	1 mile	1st	3:47.33(WR)
4 Sept	World Cup	Rome	800 m	1st	1:46.18

1982 (aged 25)

Date	Event	Venue	Distance	Place	Time
16 May	Yorkshire Championships	Cudworth	1,500 m	1st	3:39.1
5 June	International Invitation	Bordeaux	2,000 m	1st	4:58.6
4 Aug	Time Trial	Nottingham	800 m	1st	1:46.5
17 Aug	International Invitation	Zürich	800 m	1st	1:44.48
20 Aug	Talbot Games	Crystal Palace	800 m	1st	1:45.8
22 Aug	International Invitation	Cologne	800 m	1st	1:45.1
30 Aug	BAAB/Heinz Games	Crystal Palace	4 x 800 m	1st	(7:03.89)(WR)
			4th leg	1st	1:44.01
6 Sept	European Championships	Athens	800 m(h)	1st	1:48.66
7 Sept	European Championships	Athens	800 m(sf)	1st	1:47.98
8 Sept	European Championships	Athens	800 m(f)	2nd	1:46.68

1983 (aged 26)

Date	Event	Venue	Distance	Place	Time
12 Feb	GB v France (Indoor)	Cosford	1,500 m	1st	3:42.0
12 March	GB v USA (Indoor)	Cosford	800 m	1st	1:44.91(WR)
20 March	GB v Norway (Indoor)	Oslo	1,000 m	1st	2:18.58(WR)
4 April	Road Race	Vigevano	4 miles	1st	18:28
16 May	Yorkshire Championships	Cleckheaton	1,500 m	1st	3:45.01
5 June	GB v USSR	Birmingham	1 mile	1st	4:03.37
12 June	Loughborough v AAA	Loughborough	800 m	1st	1:44.99
24 June	Permit Meeting	Paris	1,500 m	2nd	3:35.17
28 June	Permit Meeting	Oslo	800 m	1st	1:43.80
15 July	Talbot Games	Crystal Palace	1,500 m	2nd	3:36.03
23 July	AAA Championships	Crystal Palace	1 mile	2nd	3:52.93
31 July	Gateshead Games	Gateshead	800 m	4th	1:45.31

1984 (aged 27)

Date	Event	Venue	Distance	Place	Time
31 March	Road Relay	Cranford	6 x 3½m	4th leg	
7 April	S. Counties Road Relay	Wimbledon	12-stage	5th leg	
21 April	AAA Road Relay	Sutton Coldfield	12-stage	5th leg	
12 May	GRE League/Haringey	Wolverhampton	4 x 400 m		
			2nd leg		46.74
19 May	Middx Championships	Enfield	800 m	1st	1:45.2
2 June	S. Counties Championships	Crystal Palace	1,500 m	1st	
24 June	AAA Championships	Crystal Palace	1,500 m	2nd	3:39.79
29 June	Permit Meeting	Oslo	800 m	1st	1:43.80
4 July	Beverly Baxter Meeting	Haringey	1 mile	1st	3:54.6
3 Aug	Olympic Games	Los Angeles	800 m(h)	1st	1:45.71
4 Aug	Olympic Games	Los Angeles	800 m(h)	3rd	1:46.75
5 Aug	Olympic Games	Los Angeles	800 m(sf)	1st	1:45.51
6 Aug	Olympic Games	Los Angeles	800 m(f)	2nd	1:43.64
9 Aug	Olympic Games	Los Angeles	1,500 m(h)	2nd	3:45.30
10 Aug	Olympic Games	Los Angeles	1,500 m(sf)	3rd	3:35.81
11 Aug	Olympic Games	Los Angeles	1,500 m(f)	1st	3:32.53(OR)
19 Aug	GRE League/Haringey	Haringey	1,500 m	1st	3:45.2
22 Aug	Permit Meeting	Zürich	1,500 m	1st	3:32.39

Appendix B

Evolution of World Records

800 metres

Time	Runner	Nation	Date	Place
1:51.9	Ted Meredith	USA	8.7.1912	Stockholm
1:51.6	Otto Peltzer	Germany	3.7.1926	London
1:50.6	Sera Martin	France	14.7.1928	Paris
1:49.8	Tom Hampson	GB	2.8.1932	Los Angeles
1:49.8	Ben Eastman	USA	16.6.1934	Princeton
1:49.7	Glenn Cunningham	USA	20.8.1936	Stockholm
1:49.6	Elroy Robinson	USA	11.7.1937	New York
1:48.4	Sydney Wooderson	GB	20.8.1938	Motspur Park
1:46.6	Rudolf Harbig	Germany	15.7.1939	Milan
1:45.7	Roger Moens	Belgium	3.8.1955	Oslo
1:44.3	Peter Snell	New Zealand	3.2.1962	Christchurch
1:44.3	Ralph Doubell	Australia	15.10.1968	Mexico City
1:44.3	Dave Wottle	USA	1.7.1972	Eugene
1:43.7	Marcello Fiasconaro	Italy	27.6.1973	Milan
1:43.5	Alberto Juantorena	Cuba	25.7.1976	Montreal
1:43.44	Alberto Juantorena	Cuba	21.8.1977	Sofia
1:42.33	Sebastian Coe	GB	3.7.1979	Oslo
1:41.72	Sebastian Coe	GB	10.6.1981	Florence

1,000 metres

Time	Runner	Nation	Date	Place
2:32.3	Georg Mickler	Germany	22.6.1913	Hanover
2.29.1	Anatole Bolin	Sweden	22.9.1918	Stockholm
2.28.6	Sven Lundgren	Sweden	27.9.1922	Stockholm
2:26.8	Sera Martin	France	30.9.1926	Paris
2:25.8	Otto Peltzer	Germany	18.9.1927	Paris
2:23.6	Jules Ladoumègue	France	19.10.1930	Paris
2:21.5	Rudolf Harbig	Germany	24.5.1941	Dresden
2:21.4	Rune Gustafsson	Sweden	4.9.1946	Boras
2:21.4	Marcel Hansenne	France	27.8.1948	Gothenburg
2:21.3	Olle Aberg	Sweden	10.8.1952	Copenhagen
2:21.2	Stanislav Jungwirth	Czechoslovakia	27.10.1952	Stará Boleslav
2:20.8	Mal Whitfield	USA	16.8.1953	Eskilstuna
2:20.4	Audun Boysen	Norway	17.9.1953	Oslo
2:19.5	Audun Boysen	Norway	18.8.1954	Gävle
2:19.0	Audun Boysen	Norway	30.8.1955	Gothenburg
2:19.0	István Rózsavölgyi	Hungary	21.9.1955	Tata
2:18.1	Dan Waern	Sweden	19.9.1958	Turku
2:17.8	Dan Waern	Sweden	21.8.1959	Karlstad
2:16.7	Siegfried Valentin	GDR	19.7.1960	Potsdam

2:16.6	Peter Snell	New Zealand	12.11.1964	Auckland
2:16.2	Jurgen May	GDR	20.7.1965	Erfurt
2:16.2	Franz-Josef Kemper	Germany	21.9.1966	Hanover
2:16.0	Daniel Malan	South Africa	24.6.1973	Munich
2:13.9	Rick Wohlhuter	USA	30.7.1974	Oslo
2:13.4	Sebastian Coe	GB	1.7.1980	Oslo
2:12.18	Sebastian Coe	GB	11.7.1981	Oslo

1,500 metres

Time	Runner	Nation	Date	Place
3:55.8	Abel Kiviat	USA	8.6.1912	Cambridge, Mass
3:54.7	John Zander	Sweden	5.8.1917	Stockholm
3:52.6	Paavo Nurmi	Finland	19.6.1924	Helsinki
3:51.0	Otto Peltzer	Germany	11.9.1926	Berlin
3:49.2	Jules Ladoumègue	France	5.10.1930	Paris
3:49.2	Luigi Beccali	Italy	9.9.1933	Turin
3:49.0	Luigi Beccali	Italy	17.9.1933	Milan
3:48.8	Bill Bonthron	USA	30.6.1934	Milwaukee
3:47.8	Jack Lovelock	New Zealand	6.8.1936	Berlin
3:47.6	Gunder Hägg	Sweden	10.8.1941	Stockholm
3:45.8	Gunder Hägg	Sweden	17.7.1942	Stockholm
3:45.0	Arne Andersson	Sweden	17.8.1943	Gothenburg
3:43.0	Gunder Hägg	Sweden	7.7.1944	Gothenburg
3:43.0	Lennart Strand	Sweden	15.7.1947	Malmö
3:43.0	Werner Lueg	Germany	29.6.1952	Berlin
3:42.8	Wes Santee	USA	4.6.1954	Compton
3:41.8	John Landy	Australia	21.6.1954	Turku
3:40.8	Sándor Iharos	Hungary	28.7.1955	Helsinki
3:40.8	Lásló Tábori	Hungary	6.9.1955	Oslo
3:40.8	Gunnar Nielson	Denmark	6.9.1955	Oslo
3:40.6	István Rózsavölgyi	Hungary	3.8.1956	Tata
3:40.2	Olavi Salsola	Finland	11.7.1957	Turku
3:40.2	Olavi Salonen	Finland	11.7.1957	Turku
3.38.1	Stanislav Jungwirth	Czechoslovakia	12.7.1957	Stará Boleslav
3:36.0	Herb Elliott	Australia	28.8.1958	Gothenburg
3:35.6	Herb Elliott	Australia	6.9.1960	Rome
3:33.1	Jim Ryun	USA	8.7.1967	Los Angeles
3:32.2	Filbert Bayi	Tanzania	2.2.1974	Christchurch
3:32.1	Sebastian Coe	GB	15.8.1979	Oslo
3:31.4	Steve Ovett	GB	27.8.1980	Koblenz
3:31.26	Sydney Maree	USA	28.8.1983	Cologne
3:30.77	Steve Ovett	GB	4.9.1983	Rieti

1 mile

Time	Runner	Nation	Date	Place
4:14.4	John Paul Jones	USA	31.5.1913	Cambridge, Mass
4:12.6	Norman Taber	USA	16.7.1915	Cambridge, Mass
4:10.4	Paavo Nurmi	Finland	23.8.1923	Stockholm
4:09.2	Jules Ladoumègue	France	4:10.1931	Paris
4:07.6	Jack Lovelock	New Zealand	15.7.1933	Princeton
4:06.8	Glenn Cunningham	USA	16.6.1934	Princeton
4:06.4	Sydney Wooderson	GB	28.8.1937	Motspur Park
4:06.2	Gunder Hägg	Sweden	1.7.1942	Gothenburg
4:06.2	Arne Andersson	Sweden	10.7.1942	Stockholm
4:04.6	Gunder Hägg	Sweden	4.9.1942	Stockholm
4:02.6	Arne Andersson	Sweden	1.7.1943	Gothenburg

4:01.6	Arne Andersson	Sweden	18.7.1944	Malmö
4:01.4	**Gunder Hägg**	Sweden	17.7.1945	Malmö
3:59.4	Roger Bannister	GB	6.5.1954	Oxford
3:58.0	John Landy	Australia	21.6.1954	Turku
3:57.2	Derek Ibbotson	GB	19.7.1957	London
3:54.5	Herb Elliott	Australia	6.8.1958	Dublin
3:54.4	Peter Snell	New Zealand	27.1.1962	Wanganui
3:54.1	Peter Snell	New Zealand	17.11.1964	Auckland
3:53.6	Michel Jazy	France	9.6.1965	Rennes
3:51.3	Jim Ryun	USA	17.7.1966	Berkeley
3:51.1	Jim Ryun	USA	23.6.1967	Bakersfield
3:51.0	Filbert Bayi	Tanzania	17.5.1975	Kingston
3:49.4	John Walker	New Zealand	12.8.1975	Gothenburg
3:49.0	Sebastian Coe	GB	17.7.1979	Oslo
3:48.8	Steve Ovett	GB	1.7.1980	Oslo
3:48.53	Sebastian Coe	GB	19.8.1981	Zürich
3:48.40	Steve Ovett	GB	26.8.1981	Koblenz
3:47.33	Sebastian Coe	GB	28.8.1981	Brussels

Appendix C

World Record Split-Times (with the times between each given distance in brackets)

1,500 metres

	400 m	800 m	1,000 m	1,200 m	1,500 m
Zander (1917)	59.0	2:02.0(63.0)		3:07.5(65.5)	3:54.7(47.2)
Nurmi (1924)	57.3	2:01.0(63.7)	2:33.0	3:06.0(65.0)	3:52.6(46.6)
Peltzer (1926)	61.5	2:03.0(61.5)	2:35.0	3:06.0(63.0)	3:51.0(45.0)
Ladoumègue (1930)	58.8	2:00.6(61.8)	2:33.0	3:05.0(64.4)	3:49.2(44.2)
Beccali (1933)	60.0	1:59.4(59.4)	2:32.8	3:07.0(67.6)	3:49.0(42.0)
Bonthron (1934)	61.0	2:01.2(62.0)		3:06.0(64.8)	3:48.8(42.8)
Lovelock (1936)	61.6	2:05.5(63.9)	2:36.0	3:05.4(59.9)	3:47.8(42.4)
Hägg (1941)	59.0	2:02.1(63.1)	2:33.0	3:03.5(61.4)	3:47.6(44.1)
Andersson (1943)	58.5	2:01.0(62.5)	2:31.0	3:00.8(59.8)	3:45.0(44.2)
Hägg (1944)	56.7	1:56.5(59.8)	2:27.2	2:58.0(61.5)	3:43.0(45.0)
Strand (1947)	57.8	1:59.3(61.5)	2:29.5	2:59.6(60.3)	3:43.0(43.4)
Santee (1954)	57.8	1:58.0(60.2)		2:58.0(60.0)	3:42.8(44.8)
Landy (1954)	57.9	1:57.5(59.6)	2:27.5	2:57.3(59.8)	3:41.8(44.5)
Salsola (1957)	56.8	1:57.8(61.0)	2:28.0	2:58.4(60.6)	3:40.2(41.8)
Jungwirth (1957)	54.9	1:54.2(59.3)	2:24.2	2:53.4(59.2)	3:38.1(44.7)
Elliott (1958)	57.5	1:57.5(60.0)	2:28.0	2:55.5(58.0)	3:36.0(40.5)
Elliott (1960)	58.5	1:58.2(59.3)	2:25.4	2:54.1(55.9)	3:35.6(41.5)
Ryun (1967)	60.5	1:56.0(55.5)	2:25.2	2:53.5(57.5)	3:33.1(39.6)
Bayi (1974)	54.9	1:52.2(57.3)	2:21.0	2:50.2(58.0)	3:32.2(42.0)
Coe (1979)	54.4	1:53.2(58.8)		2:49.5(56.3)	3:32.1(42.6)
Ovett (1980)	55.5	1:53.0(57.5)		2:50.7(57.7)	3:31.4(40.7)
Maree (1983)	54.62	1:52.80(58.9)		2:49.36(56.5)	3:31.24(41.9)
Ovett (1983)	54.17	1:51.67(57.5)		2:49.14(57.5)	3:30.77(41.6)

One Mile

	¼ mile	½ mile	¾ mile	1,500 m	1 mile
Lang (1865)	60.0	2:05.5(65.5)	3:14.0(68.5)		4:17.2(63.2)
George (1886)	58.2	2:01.7(63.5)	3:07.7(66.0)		4:12.7(65.0)
Taber (1915)	58.0	2:05.0(67.0)	3:13.0(68.0)	3:55.0	4:12.6(56.6)
Nurmi (1923)	60.3	2:03.2(62.9)	3:06.7(63.5)	3:53.0	4:10.4(63.7)
Ladoumègue (1931)	60.8	2:04.2(63.4)	3:08.0(63.8)	3:52.4	4:09.2(61.2)
Lovelock (1933)	61.4	2:03.6(62.2)	3:08.7(65.1)		4:07.6(58.9)
Cunningham (1934)	61.8	2:05.8(64.0)	3:07.6(61.8)		4:06.8(59.1)
Wooderson (1937)	58.6	2:02.6(64.0)	3:07.2(64.6)		4:06.4(59.2)
Hägg (1942)	59.1	2:02.0(62.9)	3:05.8(63.8)	3:50.8	4:06.2(60.3)
Hägg (1942)	57.2	2:00.2(63.0)	3:04.2(64.0)		4:04.6(60.4)
Andersson (1943)	59.4	2:00.8(61.4)	3:04.0(63.2)	3:47.4	4:02.6(58.6)
Andersson (1944)	57.1	1:56.8(59.7)	2:59.5(62.7)	3:46.0	4:01.6(62.1)
Hägg (1945)	56.7	1:59.2(62.5)	3:01.4(62.2)	3:45.4	4:01.4(60.0)

Bannister (1954)	57.5	1:58.2(60.7)	3:00.5(62.3)	3:43.0	3:59.4(58.9)
Landy (1954)	58.2	1:58.2(60.0)	2:58.4(60.2)	3:41.8	3:58.0(59.5)
Ibbotson (1957)	56.0	1:56.4(60.4)	3:00.4(64.0)	3:41.9	3:57.2(56.8)
Elliott (1958)	56.4	1:58.0(61.6)	2:59.0(61.0)	3:39.6	3:54.5(55.5)
Snell (1962)	60.7	2:00.6(59.9)	2:59.6(59.0)	3:39.3	3:54.4(54.8)
Snell (1964)	56.0	1:54.0(58.0)	2:54.0(60.0)	3:37.6	3:54.1(60.1)
Jazy (1965)	57.3	1:56.5(59.2)	2:57.4(60.9)	3:38.4	3:53.6(56.2)
Ryun (1967)	57.9	1:55.5(57.6)	2:55.3(59.8)	3:36.1	3:51.1(56.0)
Bayi (1975)	56.9	1:56.6(59.7)	2:55.3(58.7)	3:35.0	3:51.0(55.7)
Walker (1975)	56.3	1:55.5(58.2)	2:53.5(58.0)	3:34.3	3:49.4(55.9)
Coe (1979)	57.8	1:55.3(57.5)	2:53.4(58.1)	3:32.8	3:49.0(55.6)
Ovett (1980)	55.7	1:53.8(58.1)	2:51.0(57.2)	3:32.7	3:48.8(57.8)
Coe (1981)	56.5	1:54.2(57.7)	2:52.6(58.4)	3:33.3	3:48.53(56.0)
Ovett (1981)	56.6	1:54.5(57.9)	2:51.5(57.0)		3:48.40(56.9)
Coe (1981)	55.3	1:53.3(58.0)	2:51.9(58.6)	3:32.93	3:47.33(55.5)

Appendix D

Los Angeles Results

Abbreviations (in addition to those given in Appendix A)

Q–qualified	DNS–did not start
DQ–disqualified	DNF–did not finish

800 metres – Round I

Place	Lane	No.	Runner	Nation	Time
Heat 1					
1	1	754	Niang, Babacar	SEN	1:46.90 Q
2	7	773	Bile, Abdi	SOM	1:46.92 Q
3	3	520	Sabia, Donato	ITA	1:47.04 Q
4	6	430	Moutsanas, Sotirios	GRE	1:47.32 Q
5	4	89	Ramotshabi, Joseph	BOT	1:48.17
6	5	649	Titos, Andre	MOZ	1:51.73
7	2	1005	Sawny, Samuel	GRN	1:53.08
8	8	653	Gurung, Jodha	NEP	1:56.72
Heat 2					
1	8	359	Coe, Sebastian	GB	1:45.71 Q
2	1	780	Khalifa, Omar	SUD	1:45.81 Q
3	2	242	Trabado, Coloman	ESP	1:46.00 Q
4	3	508	Materazzi, Riccardo	ITA	1:46.03 Q
5	4	470	O'Sullivan, Marcus	IRL	1:46.85 Q
6	7	981	Musango, Archfel	ZAM	1:48.84
7	5	206	Acosta, Leopoldo	ECU	1:54.06
8	6	770	Molinari, Manlio	SMR	1:57.09
Heat 3					
1	6	541	Hamilton, Owen	JAM	1:46.95 Q
2	4	752	Fall li, Moussa	SEN	1:47.91 Q
3	3	920	Marshall, John	USA	1:47.99 Q
4	2	771	Aden, Jama	SOM	1:48.64
5	5	692	Pearless, Peter	NZL	1:49.95
6	1	436	Lopez–Davila, Alberto	GUA	1:54.19
	7	190	Ramirez–Caicedo, Manuel	COL	DNS
	8	820	Olamini, Vusie	SWZ	DQ
Heat 4					
1	6	909	Jones, Earl	USA	1:47.75 Q
2	4	623	Lahbi, Fawzi	MAR	1:47.81 Q
3	3	282	Dupont, Philippe	FRA	1:48.09 Q
4	5	313	Harries, Axel	FRG	1:48.92
5	2	553	Fawair, Muteb	JOR	1:53.89
6	1	866	Aziz, Ibrahim	UAE	1:54.86
	7	602	Kim, Bok–Joo	KOR	DQ

Heat 5

1	1	93	Cruz, Joaquim	BRA	1:45.66 Q
2	6	388	Ovett, Steve	GB	1:46.66 Q
3	2	438	Barr, Oslen	GUY	1:47.65 Q
4	3	227	Gonzalez, Benjamin	ESP	1:48.01
5	4	621	Rajakumar, Batulamai	MAL	1:48.19
6	7	625	Ganunga, Isaac	MAW	1:51.25
7	5	712	Figueredo, Francisco	PAR	1:52.22
8	8	798	Cruden, Siegfried	SUR	1:53.31

Heat 6

1	6	902	Gray, Johnny	USA	1:47.19 Q
2	7	38	Scammell, Pat	AUS	1:47.24 Q
3	5	790	Mayr, Marco	SUI	1:47.36 Q
4	2	4	Belkessam, Ahmed	ALG	1:47.51 Q
5	3	706	Rizvi, Meesaq	PAK	1:51.29
6	1	411	Amakye, William	GHA	1:54.80
7	4	761	Sinon, Philip	SEY	2:04.89

Heat 7

1	1	584	Koech, Edwin	KEN	1:47.11 Q
2	2	309	Ferner, Hans–Peter	FRG	1:47.55 Q
3	3	99	Guimaraes, Agberto	BRA	1:47.72 Q
4	8	479	Handelsman, Mark	ISR	1:47.90
5	7	534	Molyneaux, Jerry	IVB	1:53.23
6	6	972	Rudasingwa, Jmv	RWA	1:53.23
7	5	405	Esono Asumu, Bartolome	GEQ	2:17.29
	4	975	Moussa, Daweye	NIG	DQ

Heat 8

1	4	591	Ndiwa, Juma	KEN	1:46.73 Q
2	3	950	Wuycke, William	VEN	1:46.88 Q
3	2	855	Alouini, Mohamed	TUN	1:47.20 Q
4	1	124	Hoogewerf, Simon	CAN	1:47.74
5	8	964	Jonga, Tapfumanei	ZIM	1:49.59
6	5	1007	Oliver, Charlie	SOL	1:53.22
7	7	703	Alsharji, Barkat	OMA	2:00.38
8	6	952	Algadi, Abdulrab	YAR	2:05.90

Heat 9

1	6	585	Konchellah, Billy	KEN	1:46.27 Q
2	4	365	Elliott, Peter	GB	1:46.98 Q
3	3	91	Barbosa, Jose Luiz	BRA	1:47.12 Q
4	8	138	Roberts, Bruce	CAN	1:47.56
5	5	453	Borromeo, Charles	IND	1:51.52
6	2	14	Jones, Dale	ANT	1:51.52
7	1	348	Ceesay, Peter	GAM	1:55.35
8	7	156	Miangoto, Ousmane	CHA	1:56.02

The first 3 from each heat and 5 next fastest overall qualified for the next round
Temperature 26C 78F

800 metres – Round II

Place	Lane	No.	Runner	Nation	Time
Heat 1					
1	6	584	Koech, Edwin	KEN	1:44.74 Q
2	8	520	Sabia, Donato	ITA	1:44.90 Q
3	3	99	Guimaraes, Agberto	BRA	1:45.18 Q
4	4	365	Elliott, Peter	GB	1:45.49 Q
5	7	623	Lahbi, Fawzi	MAR	1:45.67
6	2	754	Niang, Babacar	SEN	1:45.71
7	5	430	Moutsanas, Sotirios	GRE	1:46.34
	1	242	Trabado, Coloman	ESP	DNS
Heat 2					
1	5	585	Konchellah, Billy	KEN	1:46.15 Q
2	1	780	Khalifa, Omar	SUD	1:46.33 Q
3	8	359	Coe, Sebastian	GB	1:46.75 Q
4	2	91	Barbosa, Jose Luiz	BRA	1:46.87 Q
5	4	920	Marshall, John	USA	1:47.18
6	7	508	Materazzi, Riccardo	ITA	1:47.90
7	3	4	Belkessam, Ahmed	ALG	1:48.11
8	6	790	Mayr, Marco	SUI	1:48.30
Heat 3					
1	1	93	Cruz, Joaquim	BRA	1:44.84 Q
2	8	388	Ovett, Steve	GB	1:45.72 Q
3	2	902	Gray, Johnny	USA	1:45.82 Q
4	6	950	Wuycke, William	VEN	1:46.17 Q
5	4	773	Bile, Abdi	SOM	1:46.49
6	3	541	Hamilton, Owen	JAM	1:46.74
7	5	38	Scammell, Pat	AUS	1:47.40
8	7	138	Roberts, Bruce	CAN	1:49.72
Heat 4					
1	7	909	Jones, Earl	USA	1:45.44 Q
2	2	309	Ferner, Hans-Peter	FRG	1:45.52 Q
3	3	591	Ndiwa, Juma	KEN	1:45.59 Q
4	4	752	Fall li, Moussa	SEN	1:45.71 Q
5	5	855	Alouini, Mohamed	TUN	1:45.78
6	8	470	O'Sullivan, Marcus	IRL	1:46.21
7	6	438	Barr, Oslen	GUY	1:46.97
8	1	282	Dupont, Philippe	FRA	1:48.95

The first 4 from each heat qualified for the semi-final
Temperature 27C 80F

800 metres – Semi-finals

Place	Lane	No.	Runner	Nation	Time
Heat 1					
1	2	93	Cruz, Joaquim	BRA	1:43.82 Q
2	3	584	Koech, Edwin	KEN	1:44.12 Q
3	8	909	Jones, Earl	USA	1:44.51 Q
4	1	388	Ovett, Steve	GB	1:44.81 Q
5	6	780	Khalifa, Omar	SUD	1:44.87
6	4	752	Fall li, Moussa	SEN	1:45.03
7	7	950	Wuycke, William	VEN	1:47.32
	5	365	Elliott, Peter	GB	DNS

Heat 2

1	1	359	Coe, Sebastian	GB	1:45.51 Q
2	5	585	Konchellah, Billy	KEN	1:45.67 Q
3	4	902	Gray, Johnny	USA	1:45.82 Q
4	7	520	Sabia, Donato	ITA	1:45.96 Q
5	8	309	Ferner, Hans–Peter	FRG	1:46.16
6	6	99	Guimaraes, Agberto	BRA	1:46.60
7	3	591	Ndiwa, Juma	KEN	1:48.06
8	2	91	Barbosa, Jose Luiz	BRA	1:48.70

The first 4 from each semi-final qualified for the final
Temperature 29C 82F

800 metres – Final

Place	Lane	No.	Runner	Nation	Time
1	6	93	Cruz, Joaquim	BRA	1:43.00 OR
2	3	359	Coe, Sebastian	GB	1:43.64
3	1	909	Jones, Earl	USA	1:43.83
4	4	585	Konchellah, Billy	KEN	1:44.03
5	2	520	Sabia, Donato	ITA	1:44.53
6	8	584	Koech, Edwin	KEN	1:44.86
7	5	902	Gray, Johnny	USA	1:47.89
8	7	388	Ovett, Steve	GB	1:52.28

Temperature 28C 82F

1,500 metres – Round I

Place	No.	Runner	Nation	Time
Heat 1				
1	578	Chesire, Joseph	KEN	3:38.51 Q
2	780	Khalifa, Omar	SUD	3:38.93 Q
3	510	Mei, Stefano	ITA	3:39.25 Q
4	694	Rogers, Anthony	NZL	3:39.78 Q
5	228	Gonzalez, Jose Luis	ESP	3:47.01
6	623	Lahbi, Fawzi	MAR	3:47.54
7	347	Ceesay, Paul	GAM	3:59.14
8	702	Alsharji, Amor	OMA	4:12.76
	260	Loikkanen, Antti	FIN	DNF
Heat 2				
1	302	Thiebault, Pascal	FRA	3:45.18 Q
2	359	Coe, Sebastian	GB	3:45.30 Q
3	244	Vera, Andres	ESP	3:45.44 Q
4	462	Donovan, Paul	IRL	3:45.70
5	771	Aden, Jama	SOM	3:46.80
6	855	Alouini, Mohamed	TUN	3:49.78
7	14	Jones, Dale	ANT	3:55.65
8	85	Balotlhanyi, Kgomotso	BOT	3:58.69
	438	Barr, Oslen	GUY	DNF
	952	Algadi, Abdulrab	YAR	DNS
	918	Maree, Sydney	USA	DNS

Heat 3

1	388	Ovett, Steve	GB	3:49.23 Q
2	99	Guimaraes, Agberto	BRA	3:49.26 Q
3	470	O'Sullivan, Marcus	IRL	3:49.65 Q
4	589	Muraya, Josephat	KEN	3:51.61
5	540	Guy, Gawain	JAM	3:52.04
6	515	Patrignani, Claudio	ITA	3:52.63
7	2	Aidet, Mehdi	ALG	3:53.92
8	553	Fawair, Muteb	JOR	3:59.85
	784	Deleze, Pierre	SUI	DNF
	950	Wuycke, William	VEN	DNS
	712	Figueredo, Francisco	PAR	DNS

Heat 4

1	93	Cruz, Joaquim	BRA	3:41.01 Q
2	938	Scott, Steve	USA	3:41.02 Q
3	29	Hillardt, Michael	AUS	3:41.18 Q
4	469	O'Mara, Frank	IRL	3:41.76
5	287	Gonzalez, Alex	FRA	3:42.84
6	479	Handelsman, Mark	ISR	3:45.05
7	9	Morceli, Abderrahmane	ALG	3:45.09
8	981	Musango, Archfel	ZAM	3:46.99
9	973	Allassane, Adamou	NIG	3:56.43
10	799	Rodrigues, Tito	SUR	4:02.87
	961	Zdravkovic, Dragan	YUG	DNS

Heat 5

1	219	Abascal, Jose	ESP	3:37.68 Q
2	797	Wirz, Peter	SUI	3:37.75 Q
3	305	Becker, Uwe	FRG	3:37.76 Q
4	508	Materazzi, Riccardo	ITA	3:37.95 Q
5	38	Scammell, Pat	AUS	3:39.18 Q
6	823	Igohe, James	TAN	3:39.62 Q
7	964	Jonga, Tapfumanei	ZIM	3:40.42 Q
8	625	Ganunga, Isaac	MAW	3:53.86
9	435	Garcia-Molina, Hugo-Allan	GUA	3:57.59
10	602	Kim, Bok-Joo	KOR	4:02.63
	866	Aziz, Ibrahim	UAE	DNF

Heat 6

1	362	Cram, Steve	GB	3:40.33 Q
2	941	Spivey, Jim	USA	3:40.58 Q
3	690	O'Donoghue, Peter	NZL	3:40.69 Q
4	773	Bile, Abdi	SOM	3:40.72 Q
5	577	Cheruiyot, Kipkoech	KEN	3:41.96
6	829	Wandu Namonge, Zakaria	TAN	3:45.55
7	621	Rajakumar, Batulamai	MAL	3:55.19
8	972	Rudasingwa, Jmv	RWA	3:57.62
9	761	Sinon, Philip	SEY	4:25.80
10	407	Lozano Idjabe, Diosdado	GEQ	4:34.71
	21	Ortega, Omar	ARG	DNF

The first 3 in each heat and 6 next fastest overall qualified for the semi-final
Temperature 27C 80F

1,500 metres – Semi-finals

Place	No.	Runner	Nation	Time
Heat 1				
1	219	Abascal, Jose	ESP	3:35.70 Q
2	938	Scott, Steve	USA	3:35.71 Q
3	359	Coe, Sebastian	GB	3:35.81 Q
4	578	Chesire, Joseph	KEN	3:35.83 Q
4	797	Wirz, Peter	SUI	3:53.83 Q
6	694	Rogers, Anthony	NZL	3:36.48 Q
7	508	Materazzi, Riccardo	ITA	3:36.51 Q
8	29	Hillardt, Michael	AUS	3:38.12
9	302	Thiebault, Pascal	FRA	3:40.96
10	823	Igohe, James	TAN	3:41.57
11	99	Guimaraes, Agberto	BRA	DNF
12	773	Bile, Abdi	SOM	DQ
Heat 2				
1	362	Cram, Steve	GB	3:36.30 Q
2	941	Spivey, Jim	USA	3:36.53 Q
3	244	Vera, Andres	ESP	3:36.55 Q
4	388	Ovett, Steve	GB	3:36.55 Q
5	780	Khalifa, Omar	SUD	3:36.76 Q
6	305	Becker, Uwe	FRG	3:37.28
7	510	Mei, Stefano	ITA	3:37.96
8	690	O'Donoghue, Peter	NZL	3:38.71
9	470	O'Sullivan, Marcus	IRL	3:39.40
10	38	Scammell, Pat	AUS	3:40.83
11	964	Jonga, Tapfumanei	ZIM	3:41.80
	93	Cruz, Joaquim	BRA	DNS

The first 4 from each semi-final and 4 next fastest overall qualified for the final
Temperature 24C 75F

1,500 metres – Final

Place	No.	Runner	Nation	Time
1	359	Coe, Sebastian	GB	3:32.53 OR
2	362	Cram, Steve	GB	3:33.40
3	219	Abascal, Jose	ESP	3:34.30
4	578	Chesire, Joseph	KEN	3:34.52
5	941	Spivey, Jim	USA	3:36.97
6	797	Wirz, Peter	SUI	3:36.97
7	244	Vera, Andres	ESP	3:37.02
8	780	Khalifa, Omar	SUD	3:37.11
9	694	Rogers, Anthony	NZL	3:38.98
10	938	Scott, Steve	USA	3:39.86
11	508	Materazzi, Riccardo	ITA	3:40.74
	388	Ovett, Steve	GB	DNF

Temperature 24C 75F

Appendix E

Olympic Games Medallists 1896–1984

Abbreviations (in addition to those given in Appendix A & D)
dna–distance not available

800 metres (874yd 2ft)

	Gold	Silver	Bronze
1896	Edwin H. Flack (AUS/NZL) 2:11.0	Nándor Dáni (HUN) 2:11.8	Demitrios Golemis (GRE) 100 yd
1900	Alfred E. Tysoe (GBR) 2:01.2	John F. Cregan (USA) 1 yd	David C. Hall (USA) dna
1904	James D. Lightbody (USA) 1:56.0 OR	Howard V. Valentine (USA) 2 yd	Emil W. Breitkreutz (USA) dna
1906	Paul H. Pilgrim (USA) 2:01.5	James D. Lightbody (USA) 2:01.6	Wyndham Halswell (GBR) 2:03.0
1908	Melvin W. Sheppard (USA) 1:52.8 OR	Emilio Lunghi (ITA) 1:54.2	Hanns Braun (GER) 1:55.4
1912	James E. Meredith (USA) 1:51.9 OR	Melvin W. Sheppard (USA) 1:52.0	Ira N. Davenport (USA) 1:52.0
1920	Albert G. Hill (GBR) 1:53.4	Earl W. Eby (USA) 1 yd	Bevil G. d'U. Rudd (SAF) dna
1924	Douglas G. A. Lowe (GBR) 1:52.4	Paul Martin (SUI) 1:52.6	Schuyler C. Enck (USA) 1:53.0
1928	Douglas G. A. Lowe (GBR) 1:51.8 OR	Erik Byléhn (SWE) 1:52.8	Hermann Engelhardt (GER) 1:53.2
1932	Thomas Hampson (GBR) 1:49.7 OR	Alexander Wilson (CAN) 1:49.9	Philip A. Edwards (CAN) 1:51.5
1936	John Y. Woodruff (USA) 1:52.9	Mario Lanzi (ITA) 1:53.3	Philip A. Edwards (CAN) 1:53.6
1948	Malvin G. Whitfield (USA) 1:49.2 OR	Arthur S. Wint (JAM) 1:49.5	Marcel Hansenne (FRA) 1:49.8
1952	Malvin G. Whitfield (USA) 1:49.2 OR	Arthur S. Wint (JAM) 1:49.4	Heinz Ulzheimer (GER) 1:49.7
1956	Thomas W. Courtney (USA) 1:47.7 OR	Derek J. N. Johnson (GBR) 1:47.8	Audun Boysen (NOR) 1:48.1
1960	Peter G. Snell (NZL) 1:46.3 OR	Roger Moens (BEL) 1:46.5	George E. Kerr (BWI) 1:47.1
1964	Peter G. Snell (NZL) 1:45.1 OR	William Cothers (CAN) 1:45.6	Wilson Kiprugut (KEN) 1:45.9
1968	Ralph D. Doubell (AUS) 1:44.3 OR	Wilson Kiprugut (KEN) 1:44.5	Thomas F. Farrell (USA) 1:45.4
1972	David J. Wottle (USA) 1:45.9	Evgeni Arzhanov (URS) 1:45.9	Michael Boit (KEN) 1:46.0
1976	Alberto Juantorena (CUB) 1:43.5 OR	Ivo Van Damme (BEL) 1:43.9	Richard Wohlhuter (USA) 1:44.1

1980 Steven Ovett	Sebastian Coe	Nikolai Kirov
(GBR) 1:45.4	(GBR) 1:45.9	(URS) 1:46.0
1984 Joaquim Cruz	Sebastian Coe	Earl Jones
(BRA) 1:43.00 OR	(GBR) 1.43.64	(USA) 1:43.83

The performances listed below were Olympic Records set additionally in the preliminaries

2:10.0	Flack	1896	1:47.1	Kerr	1960	1:46.1	Kiprugut	1964
1:59.0	Hall	1900	1:46.1	Kerr	1964			

1,500 metres (1,640yd 1ft)

	Gold	*Silver*	*Bronze*
1896	Edwin H. Flack	Arthur Blake	Albin Lermusiaux
	(AUS/NZL) 4:33.2 OR	(USA) dna	(FRA) dna
1900	Charles Bennett	Henri Deloge	John Bray
	(GBR) 4:06.2 OR	(FRA) 2 yd	(USA) dna
1904	James D. Lightbody	W. Frank Verner	Lacey E. Hearn
	(USA) 4:05.4 OR	(USA) dna	(USA) dna
1906	James D. Lightbody	John McGough	Kristian Hellström
	(USA) 4:12.0	(GBR/IRL) 4:12.6	(SWE) 4:13.4
1908	Melvin W. Sheppard	Harold A. Wilson	Norman F. Hallows[1]
	(USA) 4:03.4 OR	(GBR) 4:03.6	(GBR) 4:04.0
1912	Arnold N. S. Jackson[2]	Abel R. Kiviat	Norman S. Taber
	(GBR) 3:56.8 OR	(USA) 3:56.9	(USA) 3:56.9
1920	Albert G. Hill	Philip J. Baker[2]	M. Lawrence Shields
	(GBR) 4:01.8	(GBR) 4:02.4	(USA) dna
1924	Paavo J. Nurmi	Willy Schärer	Henry B. Stallard
	(FIN) 3:53.6 OR	(SUI) 3:55.0	(GBR) 3:55.6
1928	Harri E. Larya	Jules Ladoumègue	Eino Purje
	(FIN) 3:53.2 OR	(FRA) 3:53.8	(FIN) 3:56.4
1932	Luigi Beccali	John F. Cornes	Philip A. Edwards
	(ITA) 3:51.2 OR	(GBR) 3:52.6	(CAN) 3:52.8
1936	John E. Lovelock	Glenn Cunningham	Luigi Beccali
	(NZL) 3:47.8 OR	(USA) 3:48.4	(ITA) 3:49.2
1948	Henry Eriksson	Lennart Strand	Willem F. Slijkhuis
	(SWE) 3:49.8	(SWE) 3:50.4	(HOL) 3:50.4
1952	Josef Barthel	Robert E. McMillen	Werner Lueg
	(LUX) 3:45.1 OR	(USA) 3:45.2	(GER) 3:45.4
1956	Ron Delany	Klaus Richtzenhain	John M. Landy
	(IRL) 3:41.2 OR	(GER) 3:42.0	(AUS) 3:42.0
1960	Herbert J. Elliott	Michel Jazy	István Rózsavölgyi
	(AUS) 3:35.6 OR	(FRA) 3:38.4	(HUN) 3:39.2
1964	Peter G. Snell	Josef Odlozil	John Davies
	(NZL) 3:38.1	(TCH) 3:39.6	(NZL) 3:39.6
1968	H. Kipchoge Keino	James R. Ryun	Bodo Tümmler
	(KEN) 3:34.9 OR	(USA) 3:37.8	(GER) 3:39.0
1972	Pekka Vasala	H. Kipchoge Keino	Rodney Dixon
	(FIN) 3:36.3	(KEN) 3:36.8	(NZL) 3:37.5
1976	John Walker	Ivo Van Damme	Paul Heinz Wellmann
	(NZL) 3:39.2	(BEL) 3:39.3	(GER) 3:39.3
1980	Sebastian Coe	Jurgen Straub	Steven Ovett
	(GBR) 3:38.4	(GDR) 3:38.8	(GBR) 3:39.0
1984	Sebastian Coe	Steve Cram	Jose Abascal
	(GBR) 3:32.53 OR	(GBR) 3.33.40	(ESP) 3:34.30

[1] The Olympic record has only been set in those winning performances marked OR with the exception of Hallows, who achied 4:03.4 in the 1908 preliminaries
[2] A. N. S. Jackson (1912) changed name to A. N. S. Strode-Jackson and P. J. Baker (1920) changed named to P. J. Noel-Baker

Index